D1153237

Carnegie Commission on Higher Education
Sponsored Research Reports

ALTERNATIVE METHODS OF FEDERAL
FUNDING FOR HIGHER EDUCATION
Ron Wolk

INVENTORY OF CURRENT RESEARCH ON
HIGHER EDUCATION 1968
Dale M. Heckman and Warren Bryan Martin

The following reprints and technical reports are available from the Carnegie Commission on Higher Education, 1947 Center Street, Berkeley, California 94704.

. . . AND WHAT PROFESSORS THINK: ABOUT STUDENT PROTEST AND MANNERS, MORALS, POLITICS, AND CHAOS ON THE CAMPUS, *by Seymour Martin Lipset and Everett Carll Ladd, Jr., reprinted from* PSYCHOLOGY TODAY, *November 1970.*

DEMAND AND SUPPLY IN U.S. HIGHER EDUCATION: A PROGRESS REPORT, *by Roy Radner and Leonard S. Miller, reprinted from* AMERICAN ECONOMIC REVIEW, *May 1970.*

THE UNHOLY ALLIANCE AGAINST THE CAMPUS, *by Kenneth Keniston and Michael Lerner, reprinted from* NEW YORK TIMES MAGAZINE, *November 8, 1970, pp. 28–86.*

PRECARIOUS PROFESSORS: NEW PATTERNS OF REPRESENTATION, *by Joseph W. Garbarino, reprinted from* INDUSTRIAL RELATIONS, *vol. 10, no. 1, February 1971.*

RESOURCES FOR HIGHER EDUCATION: AN ECONOMIST'S VIEW, *by Theodore W. Schultz, reprinted from* JOURNAL OF POLITICAL ECONOMY, *vol. 76, no. 3, University of Chicago, May/ June 1968. (Out of print.)*

INDUSTRIAL RELATIONS AND UNIVERSITY RELATIONS, *by Clark Kerr, reprinted from* PROCEEDINGS OF THE 21ST ANNUAL WINTER MEETING OF THE INDUSTRIAL RELATIONS RESEARCH ASSOCIATION, *pp. 15–25. (Out of print.)*

NEW CHALLENGES TO THE COLLEGE AND UNIVERSITY, *by Clark Kerr, reprinted from Kermit Gordon (ed.),* AGENDA FOR THE NATION, *The Brookings Institution, Washington, D.C., 1968. (Out of print.)*

PRESIDENTIAL DISCONTENT, *by Clark Kerr, reprinted from David C. Nichols (ed.),* PERSPECTIVES ON CAMPUS TENSIONS: PAPERS PREPARED FOR THE SPECIAL COMMITTEE ON CAMPUS TENSIONS, *American Council on Education, Washington, D.C., September 1970. (Out of print.)*

STUDENT PROTEST—AN INSTITUTIONAL AND NATIONAL PROFILE, *by Harold Hodgkinson, reprinted from* THE RECORD, *vol. 71, no. 4, May 1970. (Out of print.)*

WHAT'S BUGGING THE STUDENTS?, *by Kenneth Keniston, reprinted from* EDUCATIONAL RECORD, *American Council on Education, Washington, D.C., Spring 1970. (Out of print.)*

THE POLITICS OF ACADEMIA, *by Seymour Martin Lipset, reprinted from David C. Nichols (ed.),* PERSPECTIVES ON CAMPUS TENSIONS: PAPERS PREPARED FOR THE SPECIAL COMMITTEE ON CAMPUS TENSIONS, *American Council on Education, Washington, D.C., September 1970. (Out of print.)*

Credit for College

Credit for College

PUBLIC POLICY FOR STUDENT LOANS

by *Robert W. Hartman*

Research Associate, The Brookings Institution

A Report for
The Carnegie Commission on Higher Education

MCGRAW-HILL BOOK COMPANY

New York St. Louis San Francisco Düsseldorf
London Sydney Toronto Mexico Panama
Johannesburg Kuala Lumpur Montreal
New Delhi Rio de Janeiro Singapore

*The Carnegie Commission on Higher Education,
1947 Center Street, Berkeley, California 94704,
has sponsored the preparation of this report as
part of a continuing effort to obtain and present
significant information for public discussion.
The views expressed are those of the author.*

CREDIT FOR COLLEGE
Public Policy for Student Loans

Library of Congress catalog card number 75-158058
123456789MAMM7987654321

07-010030-6

Contents

Foreword

The Carnegie Commission has taken a deep interest in loan programs. In our first report, *Quality and Equality,* December, 1968, we called for a "widely available student loan program in which need is not a condition of eligibility." Subsequently, in June, 1970, in a supplement to *Quality and Equality,* we proposed the creation of a National Student Loan Bank.

In the course of our discussion of alternative loan programs, we became increasingly impressed with both the prospective importance and the actual complexity of loan arrangements. We asked The Brookings Institution to undertake a careful study for us. This book, by Robert Hartman, is the result. It is the most complete and analytical study of the subject ever made.

The Brookings Institution also organized a conference, held in April, 1970, to discuss the subject. Thirty-five economists, bankers, educators, and government officials attended. The deliberations of that conference were helpful in the completion of this book. Joseph Pechman, director of economic studies at Brookings, chaired the conference and gave general guidance to the project.

The study was financed by funds from the Carnegie Commission and by a grant from the Carnegie Corporation of New York to The Brookings Institution. The views expressed in this book are those of the author and do not necessarily reflect the views of the trustees, officers, or other staff members of The Brookings Institution, the Carnegie Commission, or the Carnegie Corporation.

The issue of student loans is now under discussion within institutions of higher education as never before. It is also attracting increasing attention by the several states and by the federal government. Given the financial restraints now facing higher education specifically and governmental authorities generally, the attention given to student loans can only increase substantially. *Credit for*

College will greatly enlighten policy deliberations and greatly aid the drafting of concrete proposals.

Clark Kerr

Chairman
The Carnegie Commission
on Higher Education

May, 1971

Credit for College

Acknowledgments

The author received many helpful comments on several drafts of this study from Henry Aaron, André Danière, Harvey Galper, Martin Kramer, Roger Noll, Joseph Pechman, Alice Rivlin, Edward Sanders, Virginia Smith, and Jeffrey Weiss. Mary von Euler and Evelyn Fisher checked the text and improved the exposition. Cheerful secretarial assistance was rendered by Mary Hopkins and Sherrie Rummell.

1. *Introduction*

Students have been borrowing for generations from banks or individuals or colleges to finance their higher education, but, until recently, the volume of such transactions was small and there was no significant government involvement in loans to students. Beginning in the late 1950s, however, student borrowing increased, and both the state and federal governments entered the picture. In New York and Massachusetts, state-guaranteed agencies were established to insure and partially to subsidize private loans to students. In 1958, Congress passed the National Defense Education Act (NDEA), Title II of which provided for long-term, low-interest loans to students, with direct federal provision of most of the capital. The Higher Education Act of 1965 broadened the federal government's involvement by establishing federal assistance to state loan-guarantee agencies and by offering a program of federal loan insurance in states where students were denied access to guaranteed loans.

In the last 10 years, student borrowing under federally supported programs has increased rapidly. Under the National Defense Student Loan program, the number of borrowers has more than tripled from the first full-year level of 115,000. Annual loan volume under this program increased almost fivefold in the 1960s. In the first full fiscal year (1966–67) of the federal Guaranteed Loan Program, 330,000 students borrowed about $250 million. By 1970–71, over a million students are expected to borrow about $950 million.

Even with the rapid growth in student loans, the percentage of students who actually borrow is still relatively small, and average amounts borrowed are not large relative to the total cost of higher education. By 1970–71, full-time enrollment in colleges and universities will be about 5 million students. In addition there will be over 2 million part-time students and a substantial number of per-

1

sons attending postsecondary vocational schools, many of whom are eligible for one of the federal programs. At the most, then, perhaps one-fifth of the eligible population is participating in the federally supported loan programs. The average annual loan in these programs is well under $1,000. Relative to student charges and the incremental living costs of attending college, the average loan represents perhaps half of the cost of attending a two-year public college and less than one-fifth of the student costs of attending an expensive private college. Relative to the actual costs incurred by institutions of higher education, these ratios would be even lower; student loans are not a major financial contributor to higher education.

Some people view rapid growth of student borrowing as alarming, and some view it as encouraging. The question of how much reliance should be put on student loans in the future has become a major policy question in discussions of financing higher education. Should student loans become a major (or even the sole) mechanism to finance higher education? Or are we already burdening students with too much debt? What should be the role of the federal government in the student loan market? Should it continue existing programs? Should it facilitate the flow of capital to student loans by establishing federal lending authority or by providing a secondary market for student loan paper? Should it increase subsidies to lenders or to borrowers, or should it reduce them?

DESIRABILITY OF STUDENT LOANS Responsible people take a wide range of positions on the desirable role of student loans in higher education finance. Views on student loans, in large part, reflect the relative importance various observers attach to three basic rationales for government intervention in higher education. These rationales are:

1 *Student loans are a means for providing a general subsidy to encourage the growth of higher education.*

One reason for government intervention in higher education is that in a market economy, whenever total benefits to society exceed the benefits appropriable by the consumer ("private benefits"— higher present and future incomes), there will be a tendency for too little higher education to be produced. Students and their families will ignore the "external benefits" (such as better citizenship and leadership in politics and the arts)[1] and will tend to base

---

[1] For a denial that the existence of these benefits has been demonstrated, see Friedman (1968, p. 108).

their purchases of higher education only on the private benefits expected. This underestimation of total benefits establishes a case for government intervention: The role of government is to use tax revenues to pay that part of the cost of education which results in external benefits. The subsidy to education will lower the cost to the student-consumer so that his volume of purchase will be expanded up to the point where both private and external benefits are reflected in the decision.

Under some circumstances, loans to students in higher education can be made into a convenient vehicle for serving this objective. If all higher education institutions charged prices fully compensating them for resources purchased, the net price to the student-borrower could be lowered through the now familiar mechanisms of delayed repayment and/or below market repayment rates on loans. Although nonloan alternatives (for example, direct public subsidy of costs) are also available for meeting this objective, advocates of greater reliance on loans point to its payoff on freeing colleges to set their own priorities (rather than depending on those of state and federal legislatures, philanthropic groups, and so forth), to foster competition in education, and to protect the private university sector.[2]

2   *Student loans are a means to stimulate enrollments of certain target groups or to stimulate particular types of training.*

The public interest in providing more education than students from low-income families might be willing to purchase stems from several rationales. First is the notion that equal attainment of education by persons from varying backgrounds is a good in itself, to be evaluated alongside such other national goals as the size of the gross national product, personal freedom, and so on. Second is the view that greater equality of educational attainment may be an effective means to provide greater future equalization of incomes (Thurow, 1969*b*, chap. 5). Finally, equalization of enrollment rates can be defended as a case of what Musgrave (1959, pp. 13, 14) calls *merit wants:* the imposition of a better-informed group's preferences (for higher education) on a less-informed group.

Whatever the justification for changing the distribution of who enters and continues higher education, the evidence is quite convincing that youngsters from poor families (even holding ability

[2] See Panel on Educational Innovation (1967, pp. 5–6); Friedman (1968, p. 111); and U.S. Department of Health, Education, and Welfare (1969*c*, pp. 3–4, 37–38).

constant) are not well represented in the halls of academe (U.S. Department of Health, Education, and Welfare [HEW], 1969c, pp. 4–7; and Segal, 1969, pp. 135–144). Moreover, those low-income youth who do attend are concentrated in large measure at lower-cost and probably low-quality institutions (Hansen & Weisbrod, 1969, chap. 4; Craeger, Astin, Boruch, & Bayer, 1968).

Loans for low-income students—especially subsidized loans—are one means of attempting to alter the distribution of college attendants and graduates. Such a justification has been made for loan programs as disparate as the Educational Opportunity Bank (Panel on Educational Innovation, 1967) and the National Defense Student Loan program.[3]

Here, again, alternatives to loans are clearly available. Although no conclusive cost-effectiveness studies have been completed, a number of recent studies have advocated massive direct *grant* programs for students from families with strong financial need (Carnegie Commission, 1968; HEW, 1969c). Others have argued that direct institutional support can bring about a greater equalization of opportunity.[4]

Another target group towards which loan programs have been directed embraces students preparing for a specific occupation (for example, in the health professions) or persons actually working in a target field (for example, teachers with NDEA loans whose repayments were cancelled). The public policy interest in such programs would seem to stem from a failure of private-market wage incentives to work fully or quickly enough. In order to close a manpower gap quickly, special incentives for certain occupations can be built into loan programs through discriminating subsidies.

3 *Government intervention in student loans represents a means for compensating for failures in the private capital market to finance adequately ventures involving high private risk.*

Student loans are risky in two fundamental ways. To the lender, an educational loan, unlike house mortgages or auto loans, finances the purchase of an asset (human capital) which cannot be repossessed in case of default. But like houses and cars, education

[3] See testimony of Peter P. Muirhead, Associate Commissioner for Higher Education, in *Higher Education Amendments of 1968* (1968, p. 19).
[4] See Wolk (1968, Appendix 1d, p. 103ff.) for the statement of the American Association of State Colleges and Universities and the National Association of State Universities and Land-grant Colleges.

yields a flow of income over a long period of time and thus gives rise to a need for loan finance. In the absence of government intervention, education loans would be put at a disadvantage relative to other types of lending; lenders would try to compensate for their inability to repossess by imposing premium interest rates and/or insisting on a propertied cosigner. These extra tests are not necessarily required for noneducational loans, so the private-market process would result in an underfinancing of human capital relative to physical capital.

The provision of direct loans by the government is a straightforward corrective to the kind of imbalance induced by the special nature of educational loans. Similarly, by guaranteeing student loans against default, the government may put human capital on an equivalent footing with physical capital. Both of these techniques are now in force, and the general justification for government intervention just discussed is by far the most widely accepted in the literature.

Less generally accepted is government intervention to compensate for the second aspect of risk associated with investment in human capital. Although investment in human capital can be shown to have a fairly high average rate of return (in the form of increased earnings) to the individual (Becker, 1964, chaps. 4 and 5), there is considerable variability in these income returns. Thus, an individual contemplating an investment in college training faces a distribution of probable outcomes and the prospect that he might wind up at the lower end of the distribution. The possibility of such an unfavorable outcome, depending on how heavily the individual evaluates the disutility of a large debt burden, induces him to invest less in his education than would seem warranted from a social point of view. In private markets, institutions have arisen to allow risks of this type to be shifted: insurance, for example, is a case of a group of individuals pooling the risk of fire, death, disability, and so forth, so that no one individual need bear the full weight of risk himself (Arrow, 1965, pp. 45–56). No such institution has arisen to allow investors in human capital to pool their risks. Some proponents of student loan programs have argued that a national loan bank, issuing loans in which repayments are contingent upon future income, can provide the kind of mutualization of risk the market is unwilling to provide. Other proponents have advocated changes in the tax system to overcome the hypothesized reluctance of youth to borrow for increased future earning power.

Almost everyone would agree that higher education has some private and some external benefits. People who go to colleges and universities benefit from the experience—both financially and in other ways—and the nation as a whole benefits from having highly educated people in the population. None of these benefits, however, is exactly measurable, and people differ in their views of the relative importance of private and public benefits.

Some people are primarily impressed by the private benefits of higher education, especially those reflected in the money incomes of graduates and former students. Those who emphasize the private benefits see no reason why the taxpayer should subsidize education. They would offer higher education for sale to those who wish to purchase it at a price reflecting its cost.

If one takes this extreme position of treating higher education like other private goods, then the main problem about higher education finance seems to be the fact that higher education costs are incurred in a large lump early in life, while the benefits occur over a much longer period. Hence, people will be reluctant to buy higher education unless they can borrow to finance the cost and repay the loan over a long period. Loan markets have enabled consumers to finance the purchase of housing and other similar items over time; why not higher education?

Viewing the benefits of higher education as *entirely* private is an extreme position. At the other extreme, some people regard the private returns of higher education as unimportant compared to the public benefits which flow from having a high proportion of the population educated beyond high school. The public benefits of higher education are hard to measure, but they are thought to include higher levels of invention and scientific progress, improved cultural levels, more intelligent voting behavior, and so forth. Those who especially value the public benefits contend that leaving higher education finance to the marketplace, forcing students to bear the full cost of their own education (even on credit), will lead to serious underspending for higher education. If students have to pay any substantial part of the cost themselves, they will undertake less higher education than would be in the interest of the community as a whole.

Those who see the benefits of higher education as primarily external to the student feel that the public should bear the major cost of higher education as it does for elementary and secondary education, either by providing free public higher education to all or by providing students with direct grants to enable them to pay the cost of higher education. People who take this general position usually oppose all student loan programs. They feel that low-income students will be discouraged from obtaining higher education if they have to borrow, and they regard it as unfortunate to burden any student at the beginning of his career with educational debt.

Actually, relatively few people take either the extreme view that higher education should be totally unsubsidized or the view that it should be totally subsidized. Historically, a mixed system of higher education support has evolved in the United States for both public and private institutions. It involves some reliance on student charges. It also involves public subsidies both to institutions and to students. The present debate over the finance of higher education is not over whether there should be any subsidies at all but how great they should be, what form they should take, and who should benefit from them.

ADVANCING THE DISCUSSION No attempt is made in this report to resolve the major conflicts over the extent of subsidy in higher education or the proportion of subsidy that should go to students. Rather, the attempt is made to clarify the discussion by looking at the implications of various alternatives.

In Chapter 2, various roles for loan programs are defined, roles ranging from very modest use of loans to supplement other sources of support for higher education to reliance on loans to finance full institutional costs (net of research). What volume of loans might be expected under these alternative roles and what these volumes would do to the repayment obligations of students are shown.

The subject of discussion in Chapter 3 is the constraint on the growth of the National Defense Student Loan program imposed by the treatment of direct loans in the federal budget.

In Chapter 4, the recent history of the Guaranteed Loan Program is reviewed. Alternative ways in which the volume of these private loans could be expanded, including the introduction of a secondary market for student loans, are discussed.

Chapter 5 is organized around two questions: Who gets the benefits of present loan programs? Who should get them? An attempt is made to distinguish the different types of benefits that flow from student loans and to relate these to program goals. Explicit attention is paid to the role of subsidies in federal programs.

In Chapter 6, proposals for major reform in federal loan programs are dealt with. Among the proposals analyzed are changes in repayment provisions under present programs, the establishment of a national loan bank, proposals for an income-contingent repayment plan, and proposals for reform of special provisions for teacher-borrowers.

Chapter 7 is a summary of a conference of experts held at The Brookings Institution in April 1970 to discuss the issues raised in this study.

2. The Volume of Student Loans: Needs and Constraints

Many of the questions relating to the viability of existing loan programs and to the advisability of proposed loan plans can only be resolved after reference to estimates of the projected volume of the market. In this section several alternate roles are established for a national student loan program, and the loan volumes implied by the roles over the next decade are projected. The alternative roles are then assessed against measures of the burden of repayments on the borrower. Discussed in the following sections are the questions of whether the two major federal loan programs can meet the requirements of the several loan roles and what modifications are possible or necessary.

FIVE ROLES FOR LOANS Estimates have been made of the maximum aggregate and per student annual volume of loans that would be required under each of five prototype loan roles. The actual volume that would come about would depend on the specific terms under which the loans were offered and on the willingness of fund suppliers to make loans available. It seems appropriate, however, to estimate maximum volumes, if only to ascertain the orders of magnitude that we are dealing with.

Full cost One possible role for loans in higher education is to support the entire cost of instruction.[1] The implications of this role are that federal, state, and local government support would wither, tuition would rise, and the college and university system would become entirely market-oriented. Those, like Friedman, who see no social (as distinct from private) benefits stemming

[1] But not organized research. *Full cost* here does not include the earnings that a student gives up while attending college *(opportunity cost).*

from higher education would find this standard attractive.[2] Even if some subsidy for higher education were envisioned, a full-cost loan program with subsidized loans could be the answer. The appeal of full-cost loan programs to those who would take this more moderate view would again be the creation of a market-oriented higher education system, with all that such a system implies for free choice, the absence of government control, the efficient transfer of resources, and so on.

Total student charges Tuition and fees represent a little more than one-third of total instructional cost.[3] In addition, students are charged for a large share of the costs of auxiliary services associated with higher education: dormitory rooms, board, books, and so forth. Financing the total of student charges for all these activities provides another possible role for student loan programs. Under the full student-charges standard, government and private subsidies would continue, but the loan program would be ready to accommodate each student's costs of tuition, fees, room and board.[4] Total charges here include room and board charges whether or not they are explicitly paid. Thus, commuter students would be allowed to borrow rent and food money even if they lived with their parents. This standard for loans might appeal to those who accept the principles underlying present government and private subsidies but who would like to see the financial barriers created by student charges hurdled primarily with the help of loans. This approach implicitly assumes that existing subsidies (the gap between full cost and student charges) are about right and that remaining charges result primarily in private benefits to the student.

Student charges net of family ability to pay A more traditional approach to the role of student loans underlies the norm of student charges net of family ability to pay. The role of the state would be pretty much what it is now; student charges would be financed, as at present, in part by parental contributions. How-

[2] See Friedman (1968, p. 108). Friedman would probably not object to subsidies to the student that arise from private gifts to colleges—provided that they are voluntarily proffered.

[3] See O'Neill (forthcoming).

[4] Whether governments and eleemosynary sources would *in fact* maintain their support under this standard is another question.

ever, all charges above equitable parental contributions for which the student is liable would be available through loans, rather than through the present system of grants, work, accumulated student savings, extra parental contributions, and the like. Moreover, no student whose parents are willing to accept the responsibility of contributing an equitable amount need face any further financial barrier. (In the estimates prepared here, the maximum loan is set at $1,460—the average student charge in 1967–68. Loan eligibility depends on parents' inability to meet this charge.) It seems that this kind of role for loans would appeal to two groups. The first comprises those who really favor a full student-charge standard, but who would be wary of the political or banking system's ability to provide it. One way to allocate scarce funds under the full student-charges standard is to insist on a fair contribution by parents. A second group to whom this approach might seem sound consists of those who believe that loans should continue to play a small role, but feel that existing loan programs need a little boosting or redirection to play this role more adequately.

Status quo   In 1967–68, new loans issued to students under the major guarantee and direct loan programs of the federal government amounted to about *$700 million.* Ninety-four percent of this total is accounted for by U.S. Office of Education programs to be discussed in this study. The remainder is comprised of National Institutes of Health programs. The total amount represents about 5 percent of full costs, as defined below, and about 10 percent of student charges for that academic year. Many observers of higher education might find this role for loans about right. These observers can be divided into two groups: (a) those who would rather see no loans at all, but accept the current level in the absence of feasible alternatives, and (b) those to whom history— even the history of student loan programs—represents divine revelation.

Accessory aid[5]   A final standard, which is philosophically apart from those listed above, envisions student loans as a residual item in the overall finance scheme. The rationale for the total

---

[5] I am indebted to Alice Rivlin for first suggesting this role for loans to me. The plan bears some kinship to the views of Howard R. Bowen. See his "Financing Higher Education: Two Views (1)," (1968, pp. 3–11).

financing picture would run like this: Society's interests can be best served if the community provides the resources for a *minimum or basic* amount of higher education for all through direct grants to schools or to needy students. For those students who wish more than the minimum, a loan program should exist to finance charges above this basic amount.[6]

There is no attempt here to untangle some of the difficult problems in this approach (Which "community" — state, federal — takes care of the basic program? Does the basic grant go to students or to institutions?); estimates are made of the nonbasic costs to be financed through loans. An arbitrary, but defensible, assumption is that the minimum or basic plan would finance the first two years of college at a per student cost equal to student charges at public two-year colleges. The loan plan under this standard would have to support all student charges in excess of charges at two-year public institutions during students' freshman and sophomore years and total student charges thereafter.

ESTIMATED LOAN VOLUME UNDER THE ALTERNATIVE STANDARDS

Estimates of the annual loan per full-time equivalent (FTE) student and the total annual loan volume for various loan programs for 1967–68 and 1977–78 are presented in Table 1. Detailed discussions of the estimates are presented in Appendix A, where it is noted that the estimates, especially those for 1977–78, are subject to considerable error. Some of the difficulties are attributable to intractability of the data, but on a more fundamental level large changes in the financing of students in higher education would change other significant revenue sources and would probably significantly affect patterns of outlay by institutions of higher education. Short of a workable behavioral model of higher education, the expedient adopted for most of the projections was to impose on the present (and projected) structure of higher education the loan roles discussed above. The results almost certainly rank the alternatives correctly and seem to be of the correct order of magnitude.

Table 1 indicates, as might have been expected, a significant cleavage between the status quo and ability-to-pay standards and the others. The former plans limit the role of student loans both on an individual student basis and in the aggregate. It is inter-

[6] This standard for loan programs is quite similar to the role envisioned for local communities in elementary and secondary education under a "foundation plan" of support.

TABLE 1 *Eligible participants and annual costs of various student loan plans, 1967–68 and 1977–78**

	Total annual loan volume (billions of dollars)		Annual loan per participant (dollars)		Eligible participants (full-time equivalent)	
Type of loan plan	1967–68	1977–78	1967–68	1977–78	1967–68	1977–78
Full cost	13.8	32.2	2,680	4,143	5,150,000	7,772,000
Total student charges	7.5	16.8	1,460	2,155	5,150,000	7,772,000
Student charges net of family ability to pay	2.0	4.4	760	1,122	2,626,500	3,963,651
Status quo	0.7	1.6	719	1,061	992,195	1,497,321
Accessory aid	5.3	11.8	1,183	1,746	4,481,000	6,762,394

*Entry assumes all eligible participants will make full use of loan program.
SOURCE: Appendix A.

esting to note that to shift from the present structure of loans to basing loans on student charges net of family ability to pay would not involve any significant increase in the average loan to the participating student, but would more than double the number of students aided.

The three more radical programs of loans might involve massive changes either in the federal budget or in the private capital market. The maximum aggregate loan volume, in the base year of 1967–68, is 7 to 20 times the actual level. On a per student basis, present programs imply for the undergraduate career of today's fully participating average borrower a total debt of about $3,000, while the bigger programs might involve debts on the order of $12,000 for the same period of time.

With the more radical plans, as we shall see below, neither the present programs nor the nature of the federal commitment can remain unchanged. Even for the limited loan plans, it is not at all clear that the present programs will support the growing aggregate volume of loans required.

ACCUMULATED DEBT AND REPAYMENT CEILINGS Many opponents of increasing the role of student loans in higher education finance have referred to the "burdensomeness" of large debt accumulations by young families. If there were a consensus as to the borderline between "acceptable" and "burdensome" level of debt, public policy could be guided in establishing a maximum role for student loans. But there is no such consensus. There is general agreement, however, that the relevant measure of the

TABLE 2   *Annual repayment schedule for ten-year and twenty-year student loans of $3,000 and $9,000, by interest rate*

	Debt of $3,000					
	10-year repayment			20-year repayment		
Interest rate:	3 percent	7 percent	10 percent	3 percent	7 percent	10 percent
Dollars	351.69	427.13	488.24	201.65	283.18	352.38
Percent of income*	3.9	4.7	5.4	2.2	3.1	3.9

*Annual income is $9,000.
SOURCE: Derived by author.

oppressiveness of a debt is the relation between future repayments and future income. At some level, the repayment rate—the ratio of annual repayments to annual income—becomes burdensome. That level is referred to as the repayment ceiling.

Throughout this section we focus on the repayment rates and ceilings for college graduates in the first decade or so after graduation. There are several reasons for this choice. First, most of the discussion of the oppressiveness of educational loans has focused on family-formation years. Second, all existing programs are based on a maximum ten-year repayment period. Finally, to the extent that students base their decisions on future expectations, it seems likely that for many college students, the planning horizon extends no further than their mid-thirties, if only because of the uncertainty of income expectations beyond that age.

Annual repayments on education debt depend on the length of the repayment period (term) and the interest rate charged. The repayment rate (percent of annual income to be repaid) for loans for $3,000 and $9,000 are given in Table 2; $3,000 represents four undergraduate years at $750 per year, about the present average student loan. A $9,000 debt would result if students borrowed about $1,500 a year (full charges) for six years. Repayment rate estimates were made for an annual income of $9,000, which is roughly the median family income in 1966 of college graduates in the age bracket 25–34.[7] The family is considered the relevant economic unit.

Loan terms of 10 years and 20 years were employed for illustrative purposes, the former representing most present loan programs and the latter a rough mean of some recent proposals.[8]

[7] See Table 4, p. 21.
[8] See Danière (1969, pp. 556–598); HEW (1969c); and Shell, Fisher, Foley, & Friedlaender (1968, pp. 2–45).

Debt of $9,000					
10-year repayment			*20-year repayment*		
3 percent	*7 percent*	*10 percent*	*3 percent*	*7 percent*	*10 percent*
1,055.07	1,281.40	1,464.71	604.94	849.54	1,057.14
11.7	14.2	16.3	6.7	9.4	11.7

Unless otherwise indicated, all loans are assumed to be repaid in equal annual installments.

Three interest rates were used in the comparison: 3 percent, 7 percent, and 10 percent.[9] For a $3,000 total family debt, representing about what one average student would accumulate in four years under the more limited loan roles, the annual repayment rates range from 2.2 percent to 5.4 percent of the assumed $9,000 income. If $6,000 of debt were accumulated during college, the rates would be doubled for the $9,000 income family, ranging from 4.5 percent to 10.8 percent.

Table 2 also shows the repayment rates for a more ambitious loan plan, one in which a $9,000 debt is accumulated—which might arise as a result of heavier borrowing by one member of the family, longer schooling, or two borrowers in the family. Repayment rates for this volume of accumulated debt range from 6.7 percent to 16.3 percent per annum for the $9,000 income family.

Are these rates burdensome? Although no general consensus exists as to what a young family can afford by way of repayments, a number of suggestions have been made for assessing burdens.

Danière (1969, pp. 576ff.) has suggested that 7.5 percent of disposable income represents a socially acceptable repayment ceiling. He reaches this number by the following chain of logic:

[9] These are meant to represent the following perspectives. Three percent is the current rate employed in the existing direct loan federal programs. Seven percent is the repayment rate embodied in the Guaranteed Loan Program legislation and was the rate most commonly charged in 1968–69. The Guaranteed Loan Program, as we shall see later, has run into trouble attracting lenders at 7 percent, even though the loans are insured by the federal government. Recent legislation allows up to a 10 percent return to lenders. In the text, "subsidized rates" mean rates under 7 percent. "Unsubsidized rates" are 7 percent or over. See Appendix B for a discussion of the use of the term *subsidy* in this study.

Families spend about 90 percent of their after-tax income on consumption, leaving 10 percent for "residual purposes." It is unreasonable to expect that all discretionary income be spent on higher education repayments, so Danière identifies three-fourths of residual income for this purpose. Thus, the burden ceiling is estimated at about 7.5 percent of after-tax income or about 6.4 percent of income before taxes.[10]

Under Danière's repayment ceilings, $3,000 in accumulated debt results in tolerable repayments regardless of the term of the loan or the interest rate charged in our illustrations (see Table 2). Even if total debts were doubled to $6,000 per family, the 10-year repayment term with subsidized interest rates, or a 20-year term without subsidy, would result in repayments that barely crack the ceiling.

For the more ambitious student loan programs which might result in a $9,000 family debt, however, the Danière standard would lead to rejection of all 10-year repayment plans, regardless of the subsidy level. The 20-year repayment scheme is within the ceiling only if loans are heavily subsidized. It is well to recall here that $9,000 debt can be accumulated in only six student-years of total student charges (for example, three for the husband and three for the wife) at 1967–68 charges. Thus, Danière's repayment ceiling would suggest that even 20-year repayment periods under the more ambitious loan programs may not be feasible unless alternative time-payment arrangements can be made.

This discussion of repayment rates and ceilings can be summarized by a diagram showing those combinations of length of repayment term and interest rates which yield annual repayments of exactly $540 (6 percent repayment ceiling on $9,000 income). The curved lines in Figure 1 show the debt levels implied by such annual repayments.

This diagram makes clear that within the context of present loan plans (10-year terms, 3 to 7 percent interest) total family debts of up to about $4,500 are compatible with the Danière repayment ceiling. However, $4,500 represents only about 3 years' worth of total student charges, so that existing programs are only compatible with limited loan roles. Expansion of repayment terms to 20 years

[10] Personal income and social security taxes represent about 15 percent of income in the $9,000 range. Thus, the ceiling 0.075 Yd, where Yd is disposable income, becomes 0.06375Y, where Y is total income and $Yd = 0.85Y$.

would increase the feasible debt to about $8,000 at subsidized rates and to about $5,500 at unsubsidized rates.

At the large debt ($9,000) end of the spectrum, the diagram illustrates the impossibility of designing an unsubsidized loan program with fixed repayment obligations compatible with the repayment ceiling. Even at 40-year terms such loans would bear interest of 5.4 percent and would require a subsidy. It is for this reason that advocates of an unsubsidized national loan bank playing a major role in higher education finance have had to devise repayment provisions that (a) involve very long-term repayments and (b) allow repayments to remain low in immediate postgraduate years. These plans will be discussed in Chapter 6.

Although this discussion has been conducted in terms of recent levels of income of college graduates and in terms of current student charges, the discussion applies equally well to the future, under reasonable assumptions. For example, if young college graduate families should earn 50 percent more in a decade, our annual repayment ceiling would rise by 50 percent. This would have the effect of shifting all the curves in Figure 1 upward and to the right. The young college graduate would be able to afford repayments on about $9,000 debt (20 years, 7 percent) rather than $6,000 as in the diagram. But the meaning of $9,000 debt will change. If student charges rise by 50 percent during the decade (see Table 1, p. 13), indebtedness of $9,000 will result from a loan program with exactly the same relative role in financing students in 1977–78 as today's loan programs that result in a $6,000 debt. Only if college graduate incomes rise faster than student charges will our repayment ceiling allow more ambitious student loan programs to be feasible at given interest rates and repayment terms. If, on the contrary, student charges rise faster than college graduate incomes, the maintenance of the repayment ceilings will require, for any given relative role of loans in higher education finance, that terms be lengthened or interest rates be reduced.

An alternative approach to finding a repayment ceiling for young college graduates is to assume that during the decade after college they might be willing to repay the entire increment in earnings attributable to their higher education in those years. Earning a bachelor's degree would still "pay" in the sense that the higher earnings of later years in life would be available to maintain a consumption spread above that of high school graduates.

In 1959, the ratio of earnings of male college graduates aged

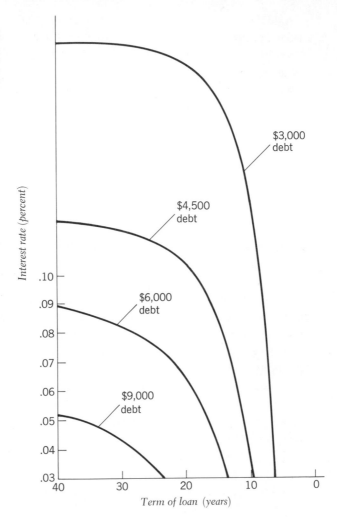

FIGURE 1
Debt levels, terms, and interest rates producing $540 annual repayments

25 to 34 to the earnings of male high school graduates in the same age group was 1.27.[11] Part of this earnings differential is probably attributable to factors other than higher education, as such. If we assume that two-thirds of the differential *is* attributable to higher education, the earnings ratio would have to be reduced to about

[11] This ratio is for Northern and Western white, nonfarm males. The ratio is slightly smaller for Northern nonwhites and considerably higher for all races in the South. These data are from Edward F. Denison (unpublished manuscript), and were derived from U.S. Bureau of the Census, 1963. (College graduate here means four or more years of college.)

1.18.[12] In other words, in the decade after graduation, a given college graduate on an average can expect to earn about 18 percent more annually than a high school graduate, solely because of his greater schooling.

Given our assumption here that college graduates might be willing to accept an annual level of repayments equal to the increment in their age 25 to 34 incomes attributable to higher education, the repayment ceiling would be about 15 percent of the typical college graduate's family income.[13] Assuming $9,000 as the typical college graduate's annual income, these estimates imply an annual repayment of $1,350. Table 3 shows the debt accumulations possible at various interest rates and repayment terms of annual repayments of $1,350.

In contrast to the conservative repayment ceilings previously estimated, these more liberal estimates suggest that even at the 10-year repayment term and interest rate (3 to 7 percent) of present programs, four undergraduate years of borrowing up to $2,000 each year results in an accumulated debt that is less than these repayment ceilings permit. Extension of repayment periods to 20 years would enable the college student to accumulate a debt in excess of his total student charges at any interest rate shown in Table 3 without exceeding the repayment ceiling in the decade after graduation. In the second decade of repayments, repayment rates would be even lower because of higher income.

To the extent that public policy for student loans should be guided by limiting the role of student loans to a level of repayment rates less than the repayment ceilings, the following conclusions are appropriate.

- A modest role for loans, resulting in debt accumulations of about $3,000, results in repayment rates well within both repayment ceilings discussed here. The ceiling is not reached even under the 10-year repayment term usually found in present federal programs.

---

[12] See also Denison (1962, pp. 67–74) and Weisbrod & Karpoff (1968, pp. 491–497). Denison assumes that 60 percent of the earnings differentials are due to schooling, while Weisbrod and Karpoff attribute about three-quarters of the difference to schooling.

[13] If the ratio of college graduate earnings (C) to high school graduate earnings (H) is 1.18, than $(C - H)/C = 0.15$. I am assuming that nonearnings income in this age bracket is negligible.

TABLE 3	*Rate and term*	*Debt level*
	3 percent	
	10 years	$11,516
	20	20,085
	30	26,461
	7 percent	
	10 years	9,482
	20	14,302
	30	16,752
	10 percent	
	10 years	8,295
	20	11,493
	30	12,726

TABLE 3
Debt levels
with annual
repayment of
$1,350, by
selected interest
rates and terms
of loans

SOURCE: Derived by author.

The repayment ceiling would not be violated even if these programs were to be unsubsidized.

• The larger debt accumulations, say $9,000, made probable under the programs emphasizing student loan finance of higher education, lead to less clear-cut conclusions. Using the more conservative 6 percent repayment ceiling implies that repayment terms would have to be extended to 30 to 40 years to finance the larger debt accumulations. Moreover, some subsidy might be required unless a larger share of the repayments could be shifted to later years. On the other hand, if repayment rates of 15 percent of income were admissible, the large debt accumulations implied by significantly increasing the role of loans in higher education finance are compatible with 10-year terms and interest rates of 7 percent or less. Lengthening repayments to 20 years would keep annual repayment rates under 15 percent for any conceivable interest rate.

THE INCOME OF COLLEGE GRADUATES All repayment rate and ceiling calculations have been based on an assumed prototypical young college graudate with $9,000 family income. Table 4 reports the actual incomes of college graduates, by age, in 1966. Our $9,000 annual income assumption holds up pretty well for that year, being somewhat too high for those under age 28 and too low for those 28 and over. If public policy toward student loans were to have been based on acceptable repayment rates for typical college graduates in the years prior to

1966, the use of a $9,000 family income as typical for young college graduates would have been reasonable.

There are, of course, many young college graduate families with incomes below $9,000. If student loan programs were expanded to limit repayment rates, not for the median young family, but rather for all but the 20 percent least successful graduates, Table 4 shows that a $5,000 to $6,000 annual income assumption would have been more appropriate for 1966. The possible repayment problems of these lower-than-average earners could perhaps be best addressed through some form of repayment insurance, as we shall see in Chapter 6.

Combining the income levels shown in Table 4 with our previous estimates of repayment ceilings leads to an inescapable conclusion with respect to the current loan programs: There have been a great many college students in recent years whose incomes upon graduation were sufficient to support substantial amounts of debt without imposing oppressive financial burdens. Have these students borrowed in such sums under either of the major U.S. Office of Education loan programs?

DEBT LEVELS UNDER EXISTING PROGRAMS The National Defense Student Loan (NDSL) program has been in existence for a decade, enough time for there to be reliable information on the total indebtedness accumulated by student borrowers under the program. This program has offered loans bearing 3 percent interest repayable over a 10-year period. At the end of fiscal year 1968, the average terminal borrower under the NDSL had accumulted a total indebtedness of $976, representing a little less than two loans of $500 (the average loan for 1959–68) each.[14] This total per student indebtedness, however, has increased recently. In fiscal year 1968, students who were in the "grace period" (that is, the year before repayments start) had accumulated an average indebtedness of $1,247, more than double the average 1965–68 loan of $550.[15]

Fragmentary data on indebtedness under the other major U.S. Office of Education program, the Guaranteed Loan Program (GLP),

---

[14] A terminal borrower is one who graduated, transferred, dropped out, died, or became bankrupt at any time since the program began. With the exception of transfers, this category corresponds to those who have completed their student borrowing.

[15] Computed from data provided by the U.S. Office of Education on operations of the National Defense Student Loan program.

		Income class					
Age of head	$0 to $2,999	$3,000 to $5,999	$6,000 to $7,499	$7,500 to $8,999	$9,000 to $11,999	$12,000 to $14,999
24–25	3.7%	26.0%	16.2%	16.8%	22.4%	9.0%
26–27	7.6	8.1	24.4	19.2	27.8	10.2
28–29	5.0	12.1	14.1	12.2	29.2	8.8
30–31	.5	18.6	11.8	13.4	21.1	18.7
32–34	3.0	6.4	12.0	12.3	30.9	18.4
35–44	2.2	4.9	7.8	7.9	26.3	20.3

TABLE 4
*Distribution of 1966 college graduate households by income class and by age of head**

* Household whose head or spouse of head is college graduate (not in school during year).

† Medians and lowest quintiles estimated by linear interpolation.

SOURCE: Machine tabulation of Survey of Economic Opportunity, February 1967, a national sample of individual and family characteristics made by the U.S. Bureau of the Census for the U.S. Office of Economic Opportunity (unpublished).

have recently become available. The borrowing frequency of a cohort of 34,966 first-time borrowers in fiscal year 1966 was followed through fiscal year 1969. Results of frequency and amounts of borrowing are shown in Table 5. On the average, the GLP participant borrowed about two times, resulting in an average indebtedness of $1,386. A preliminary estimate of the indebtedness experience of the 1967 cohort of first-time borrowers indicates that if they follow the frequency-of-borrowing pattern of their

TABLE 5
*Frequency of borrowing and average indebtedness under the Guaranteed Loan Program**

Frequency of borrowing	Number	Average debt†
1 time	17,394	$ 628
2 times	7,549	1,446
3 times	5,742	2,299
4 times	4,281	3,139
TOTAL	34,966	
Total debt		$48,478,203
Average number of times borrowed	1.91	
Average debt per borrower		$1,386

* Estimated from fiscal year 1966 cohort of first-time borrowers.

† Average debt is computed by cumulating the average first loan, second loan, and so forth, for the fiscal years 1966, 1967, and so on. The implicit assumption is that those who borrowed a second and last time in 1967, for example, took the same average loan as those who borrowed a second time in 1967 and borrowed again in subsequent years.

SOURCE: U.S. Office of Education, 1969a.

	Income	
$15,000 and over	*Median† (dollars)*	*Lowest quintile† (dollars)*
5.9%	$ 7,866	$4,881
2.7	8,273	6,264
18.5	9,678	6,309
15.8	9,810	6,114
17.0	10,583	7,325
30.6	12,133	8,468

predecessors, average indebtedness for that cohort might rise by about $200 to create a debt level between $1,500 and $1,600.

The annual repayments implied by the average levels of indebtedness under existing programs are miniscule in relation to family incomes of current college graduates. At 3 percent, 10-year repayment terms, the NDSL borrower with $1,250 indebtedness pays $147 annually, or 1.6 percent of a $9,000 family income. Even if we use the income of the parents of the students as the base — about $6,000 for the median NDSL borrower in fiscal year 1968 — the repayment rate is less than 2.5 percent.

For the GLP borrower repaying at 7 percent for 10 years, $1,500 total debt translates into $214 in annual repayments, or less than 3 percent of a $9,000 family income.[16] Even if a college graduate earned $5,000 — placing him in the lowest quintile among 25-year-old graduates in 1966 — this level of debt would require a repayment rate of under 5 percent, well below the repayment ceilings discussed above.

[16] Under the law governing the GLP, annual repayments must not be less than $360. So a student with only $1,500 total debt will actually repay $360 or 4 percent of a $9,000 family income. His repayment term would be less than 10 years in this case.

3. Constraints on Growth of National Defense Student Loans

The discussion in the preceding chapter indicated that repayment rates under existing student loan programs have hardly been excessive. If individual student demands correspond at all closely to what we have called the repayment ceiling, there must be a large unsatisfied demand for loan funds from existing programs. The volume of neither of the two major general loan programs —National Defense Student Loans and the Guaranteed Loan Program—has been limited by student demand. In the case of NDSL, congressional appropriations form the fundamental limiting factor, while the GLP's volume is determined by the interplay of federal rules and lenders' reactions to the rules. These limiting factors will be discussed individually.

THE BUDGET PROCESS AND THE NDSL PROGRAM

Over the past few years, as indicated in Table 6, the volume of loans extended under the GLP has grown at a much faster pace than those extended under the NDSL program. This trend is part of a general shift in federal government credit programs toward guarantees and insurance and away from direct loans. For example, in fiscal 1961, new commitments for direct loans in the federal budget were about $10 billion out of total (direct and guaranteed-insured) commitments of about $26 billion. By fiscal year 1972, direct loans are expected to represent only one-fifth of the total of about $58 billion in new commitments.[1] The principal reason for the shift toward guaranteed loans has been the tightness of the federal education budget. As a result of the increasing pinch on the budget, U.S. Office of Education decision makers have shifted funds out of the NDSL program in full awareness that this shift would stimulate the demand for guar-

[1] See U.S. Bureau of the Budget (1971, p. 67).

	Volume		Ratio of National
Fiscal year	*National Defense Student Loans*	*Guaranteed Loans*	*Defense Student Loans to Guaranteed Loans*
1966	$214.3	$ 77	2.8
1967	221.6	248	0.9
1968	233.7	436	0.5
1969	265.1*	687	0.4

TABLE 6
Loan volume of National Defense Student Loan and Guaranteed Loan programs, fiscal years 1966–69 (dollar amounts in millions)

*Estimate.
SOURCES: NDSL, 1966–1968: U.S. Office of Education, "NDSL Operations Summary" (unpublished); GLP, 1966–1968: U.S. Office of Education, 1969b; NDSL, 1969: U.S. Department of Health, Education, and Welfare, *Budget Estimates, Fiscal Year 1970,* vol. VI, p. 70–77; GLP, 1969; *The Budget of the United States Government, Fiscal Year 1971,* 1970, Appendix, p. 433.

anteed loans. Such a shift produces "budget-savings" because the former program appears as an item in the budget while the latter does not. Contrary to the usual rhetoric accompanying budget cuts, there is no reason to believe that such substitutions among loan programs have any net impact on real economic activity. Moreover, the impact of such shifts on the public versus private mix in the economy is ambiguous, at best. Thus, recent relative reductions in the NDSL program cannot be justified by the arguments usually proffered for the cutback: namely, that the cuts were necessary to reduce inflation.

To clarify the comparison of the effects of direct versus insured loans, let us follow through in a step-by-step fashion the consequences of a new direct or insured loan.

Suppose identical twins, A and B, attend Yale. At 1:00 P.M. on a given day, A appears at the student financial aid officer's desk and requests a $100 loan to finance unanticipated laboratory fees. The financial aid officer calls Washington, obtains the commitment, and grants the loan. Between 1:00 P.M. and 2:00 P.M., the U.S. Treasury sells a $100 bond to finance the direct loan. (The unrealism of the process described here simplifies the exposition and, I hope, does no glaring injustice to the principles involved.)

At 2:00 P.M., B appears at the financial aid officer's door with the same loan request. The financial aid officer has used up his direct loan allotment for the year and calls the First Bank of New Haven to arrange a guaranteed loan for B. The loan is arranged, and the First Bank sells off $100 in United States government bonds from its portfolio to finance the transaction.

There would be general agreement that if the repayment schedules for A's and B's loans were the same, the economic effects on the two borrowers would be the same—namely enlarged consumption of laboratory materials. In this example, then, if our standard of comparison is the economic impact on the recipient, there is no difference between the direct and insured loan. The difference in opinion arises over "who really finances the loan." Some would argue that the direct loan is financed through federal borrowing, while the insured loan is financed through private credit. But this view is misleading and myopic.

In each case, the student loan is paid for in real terms by *those borrowers who are squeezed out of the market by the credit stringency caused by either loan.* A's loan places an additional demand on the capital market through the U.S. Treasury sale of a bond; B's loan creates an identical demand on the capital market by the bank's sale of a bond from its portfolio. The effects of either of these increases in demand would be an increase in interest rates—thus squeezing out some marginal borrower in the economy.

The Federal Reserve might react to rising interest rates by expanding the monetary base. If it does so, the financier of the student loan is "monetary expansion" and, in times of full employment, the loser is the general public whose real income is reduced by a higher price level. So student loans either replace borrowing for other purposes or replace consumption by the general public, *but the effect is the same for direct or insured loans.*

If the federal government becomes alarmed by the rising price levels, as it has in recent years, Congress or the President might squelch the inflationary gap by reducing other public expenditures or by raising taxes. In this case, student loans are paid for by the beneficiaries of other government programs or by the taxpaying public. *The effect is the same for guaranteed or insured loans.*[2]

Although direct and guaranteed loan programs with comparable repayment terms have precisely the same economic effects, the present budget treatments of the major U.S. Office of Edu-

---

[2] See also Break (1968, pp. 58–79). Break believes that some of the outcomes above are more likely under direct loans and that others are more likely under guaranteed loans. My position is that fiscal choices of the federal executive and legislative branches ultimately determine which activities are displaced by an enlarged student loan volume. These choices are likely to be the same, regardless of the method of loan finance.

TABLE 7 *Program information on National Defense Student Loan and Guaranteed Loan programs, fiscal years 1968 and 1969*

	National Defense Student Loans		Guaranteed Loans	
Program information	1968	1969	1968	1969
Number of borrowers	429,000	442,000	515,000	787,000
Total loan volume (millions of dollars)	233.7	265.1	435.8	687.0
Borrowers' interest rate during enrollment, military and other exempt periods (percent)	0	0	0	0
Borrowers' interest rate during repayment (percent)	3	3	3	7
Interest return to lender (percent)	6*	7*	6	7
Other benefits, teacher cancellation (millions of dollars)	20.3	n.a.†	0	0

*The National Defense Student Loan program is a direct loan program. The ultimate lender cannot be determined. The interest rate for the private Guaranteed Loan Program is used as a measure of the foregone interest in this program.
† Not available.
SOURCES: *The Budget of the United States Government, Fiscal Year 1971,* Appendix, p. 427; U.S. Department of Health, Education, and Welfare, *Budget Estimates, Fiscal Year 1970,* vol. VI, pp. 69–77 and 70–77.

cation loan programs—NDSL and GLP—are widely divergent.[3] To be sure, the repayment terms on the two programs are not the same, but this is not the reason for the variation in the federal budget.

How could the budget treatment of these programs be improved to provide more rational decision making? To answer this, it is necessary to look in some detail at the programs. Table 7 lists the major program characteristics in fiscal years 1968 and 1969, including the number of borrowers, the amount borrowed, and interest information. In fiscal year 1969, the maximum interest rate in the GLP was raised to 7 percent, but students were obligated to pay all, rather than half, of the interest cost during repayment. Both programs involve a maximum of 10 years to repay, once repayments start.

Table 8 presents information on the two loan programs as it appears in the official federal budget. The contrast in the two tables is striking. Table 7 shows that in fiscal 1968 the GLP encouraged almost twice as many dollars into student loans as did the NDSL program. But the federal budget makes the latter

[3] The health and nursing loans are similar to NDSL and raise no new issues of principle in this context.

TABLE 8
*Federal
budget
information on
National
Defense Student
Loan and
Guaranteed
Loan programs,
fiscal years
1968 and 1969*

Budget information	1968	1969
National Defense Student Loans		
Federal capital contributions (millions of dollars)	178.4	190.0
Reimbursements for teacher cancellations (millions of dollars)	1.7	1.4
TOTAL (millions of dollars)*	180.1	191.4
Budget cost per dollar of loan (dollars)†	.77	.72
Budget cost per borrower (dollars)†	420.00	433.00
Guaranteed Loans		
Advances for reserve funds (millions of dollars)	7.9	4.7
Interest payments (millions of dollars)	32.0	65.0
TOTAL (millions of dollars)	39.9	69.7
Budget cost per dollar of loan (dollars)†	0.09	0.10
Budget cost per borrower (dollars)†	77.00	89.00

*Not including loans to institutions.
†Derived by author.
SOURCES: *The Budget of the United States Government, Fiscal Year 1971,* Appendix p. 427; U.S. Department of Health, Education, and Welfare, *Budget Estimates, Fiscal Year 1970,* vol. VI, pp. 69–77 and 70–77.

program look 4½ times bigger than the former in that year. The NDSL program loan volume increased about $30 million, or 13 percent, between the two years; but the federal budget shows only a $10 million, or 6 percent, increase between the years. For the GLP, the annual growth of new loan volume was 58 percent; budget costs for that program increased even faster, rising 75 percent. These discrepancies between the actual relative sizes and growth rates of the two programs and their budgetary levels and changes stem from one factor—the "age" or state of maturity of the programs. At some later date in the programs' lives, the federal budget will show much larger charges for GLP than NDSL, and the unit cost measures of Table 8 will be reversed.

Each program's budget level in relation to program (new loan volume) level will evolve differently. In the early stages of the NDSL program, federal capital contributions—thus federal budgets—must be maintained at a high level relative to new loan volume to sustain that loan volume. At a later stage, as repayments mount, annual federal budget reductions are compatible with a growing loan volume, as the loan principal is supplied by the repayments. At "maturity" in a modestly growing NDSL program, federal budget contributions will become very small, limited to supplying a part of the annual growth in the program, as the revolving fund of repayments and interest carry the major burden of finance. By contrast, in a modestly growing interest-subsidy program of the GLP type, early years involve very small interest charges. But as the volume of outstanding loans grows, so do the interest costs. The growth in interest payments in this program levels off as repayments reduce the amount of loans outstanding. Figure 2 illustrates these trends for a direct and interest-subsidy program of equal program levels. The arrows indicate where the two U.S. Office of Education programs were in their life-span in 1970. In both cases, we assume that 1967–68 rules govern and that defaults and teacher cancellations are nil.

The program information (Table 7) shows a substantial change in the GLP between fiscal 1968 and 1969: The federal interest subsidy during the repayment period was removed in the latter year. This means that for each dollar of GLP aid in 1969, a larger amount will have to be paid back in the future. It does not seem sensible for the borrower or the decision maker to be indifferent to this kind of change in the character of the aid proffered between the two years. But the budget data do not in *any* way account for this change.

These two programs can be placed on similar footing by a "budget" procedure that adjusts for the shortcomings of the federal budget treatment: For each program, estimate the total volume of loans originated in each fiscal year. Separate the total volume of loans into "pure loans" and "subsidies due to delayed repayment and below-market interest rates."[4] Treat teacher

FIGURE 2
Trends for a direct and interest-subsidy program of equal loan program levels

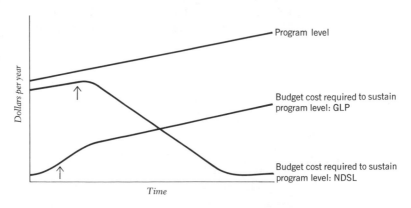

[4] See the first footnote to Table 9 for estimating procedure and Appendix B for a discussion of what subsidies mean in this context.

Type of loan	Fiscal 1968	Fiscal 1969
National Defense Student Loans		
Total volume	233.7*	265.1†
Pure loan	169.3	178.2
Subsidy	64.4	86.9
Guaranteed Loans		
Total volume	435.8*	687.0‡
Pure loan	315.7	560.6
Subsidy	120.1	126.4
Teacher cancellation§	25.7	n.a.¶

*For fiscal year 1968, the total loan volume (from Table 7) was divided into its two components as follows. The cost *to the borrower* was calculated by discounting the constant annual sum repayment stream (based on a 3 percent, 10-year repayment schedule). Repayments were assumed to begin in the fourth year after 1967–68. The discount rate employed was 6 percent, representing the market rate for student loans in this year. The discounted repayments—the "present value of repayments"—represent 72.4 percent of the principal amount of the loan. Thus, 72.4 percent of the loan volume is the present equivalent of a 6 percent loan extending for 13 years ("pure loan") while the remaining 27.6 percent is the present equivalent of the grant, or subsidy, produced by delayed repayment and low repayment interest rates.

† The same technique is used as in 1967–68, but repayments are discounted at 7 percent, the market rate in 1968–69. As a result of the higher discount rate, the subsidy ratio rises to 32.8 percent.

‡ The same technique is used as in 1967–68, but under GLP rules that came in force in 1968–69, the student was liable for all repayments (at 7 percent) during the repayment period. Thus, the subsidy per dollar of loan drops to 18.4 percent.

§ There are no firm data on the number of students from any given cohort of borrowers who will apply for teacher cancellations. In 1967, the Under Secretary of the Treasury, Joseph W. Barr (1968, p. 39), estimated that 25 percent of the loan volume will eventually be canceled at the rate of 10 percent of the principal (plus all interest) per year for the 5 consecutive years commencing with the start of the repayment period. The present value of this forgiveness feature per $1,000 of loan discounted at 6 percent is $440. Forty-four percent of one-quarter of the 1967–68 NDSL loan volume is $25.7 billion.

¶ Not available.

SOURCE: Appendix, Table C-5.

cancellations anticipated from each year's loans as expected future grants and enter, appropriately discounted, as a separate line in the "budget." The results of this revision are given in Table 9.

In contrast to the budget in Table 8, which gives the impression that the 1967–68 NDSL program was four times more costly to the government than the GLP, Table 9 indicates that in terms of subsidies implied by program levels in that year, the GLP was nearly twice as costly as the NDSL. Ignoring teacher cancellations, the two programs were equally costly per dollar of loan: 27.6 cents in subsidy for each dollar of loan. Teacher cancellations by our conservative estimates, however, add substantially to the cost of the NDSL program. For some NDSL "borrowers," those who become eligible for cancellation of the total loan, the NDSL program is simply a very complicated form of grant. There is no pure loan involved at all—the sum provided is a pure subsidy, indistinguishable from a grant.[5]

By 1968–69, the program volume had grown to $952 million. Of this total, interest subsidies represented $211 million. In the GLP the interest subsidy is entirely accounted for by the absence of any interest charge during enrollment, military service, and so forth, while in the NDSL the subsidy is also attributable to low interest during repayment. As interest rates rose from 1967–68, the subsidy value of the unchanged repayment terms of the NDSL increased. Between 1967–68 and 1968–69 the net result is that the subsidy implicit in the NDSL increased both per dollar of loan and in the aggregate, while the implicit subsidy of the GLP was significantly reduced per dollar of loan (although it is still substantial) but rose slightly in the aggregate.

Although there have been numerous discussions in congressional hearings of possibly eliminating one or another of the major loan programs, very little discussion has centered on the really critical variables. Congress should consider (a) who decides (that is, who makes the rules) whether the loan should be granted, (b) the extent of federal control over the volume of loans, (c) who gets the loans—different classes of borrowers may participate differently, and (d) which type of loan minimizes the costs of origination and collection. These issues will be discussed in Chapter 6.

As has been demonstrated in this chapter, the misleading budget treatment of the GLP and the NDSL significantly understates the full costs of the GLP relative to the NDSL. Nevertheless, there are real differences between the two programs, and these differences indicate that the subsidy element in the NDSL is larger than in the GLP. Whether for rational reasons (limiting subsidies) or irrational ones (making the budget appear smaller) it seems likely that heavy reliance will continue to be placed on the GLP. Some of the pitfalls in expanding the program are discussed in the next chapter.

[5] Note that in Table 9 the teacher-cancellation subsidy should not be added to the sum of the pure loan and interest subsidy lines. The sum of the volume lines gives "funds made available in the current year," while the sum of all the subsidy lines (including teacher cancellation) gives "present value of all gifts made in the current year."

4. Constraints on Growth of Guaranteed Loan Program

The federal program of guarantee of state and private student loans and of federally insured student loans (P.L. 89–329 [79 Stat. 1219]) was put on the law books on November 8, 1965. In the five years since the statute was enacted, there have been numerous amendments, usually debated in Congress under crisis conditions. Virtually all the amendments and the crisis atmosphere that has surrounded the program stem from one basic difficulty: an insufficient volume "to make loan funds available to all qualified students who desired to borrow."[1] As a result of the perennial claims of insufficient funds, Congress has progressively liberalized the return to lenders in this program to allow it to achieve the significant growth path revealed in Table 6.

Before discussing prospects for the future growth of the Guaranteed Loan Program, it is important to gain an understanding of how the aggregate loan volume is determined. For illustrative purposes, data for fiscal year 1969 will be used in the subsequent discussion.

In fiscal year 1969, the ceiling interest rate on loans made under the GLP was 7 percent. By the end of the fiscal year, most lenders were charging the ceiling rate, and it was clear that the loan supply of $687 million was insufficient to meet the demands of borrowers. These program attributes are summarized in the demand and supply curves illustrated in Figure 3.

At the 7 percent rate of return, lenders were willing to provide $687 million in guaranteed loans (point Z). In the diagram the supply curve, S, passes through this point. The curve slopes upward to the right, reflecting the increased willingness of lenders to divert funds into guaranteed student loans as yields on these

[1] Statement by James E. Allen, Jr. before the Special Subcommittee on Education of the Committee on Education and Labor, House of Representatives, July 29, 1969.

FIGURE 3
Demand and
supply of
guaranteed
loans

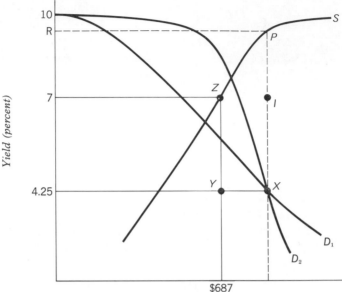

Annual volume of guaranteed loans (millions)

loans rise. As the guaranteed-loan yield approaches the yield on nonguaranteed personal loans (shown here, for illustrative purposes, as 10 percent), the supply curve of funds for guaranteed loans becomes very flat, reflecting lenders' willingness to supply funds at high yield with little or no risk of default.

The $687 million supplied was borrowed by students at an average real cost of about 4.25 percent. This rate is lower than the lender's yield because of the government's subsidization of interest during enrollment, grace period, military and other service.[2] However, there is general agreement among experts that students would have been willing to borrow more than $687 million in fiscal year 1969 at the 4.25 percent cost—point X indicates the desired borrowings at that rate (that is, X is a point on the borrowers' demand curve).[3] The gap, or insufficiency, in guaranteed loans is shown on the diagram as the distance *YX.*

[2] See Appendix B on subsidies in federal loan programs for derivation of the borrower's interest rate. The 7 percent repayment rate referred to in previous sections is the rate on which the repayment schedule is based, but does not account for the fact that no interest is charged during enrollment and military and voluntary service.

[3] If borrowers are responsive to the level of periodic payments, rather than to interest rates as such, the demand curve must be interpreted as the demand for student loans of a given repayment period (here 10 years). There will be a different demand curve for each repayment period of different length.

One of the factors crucial to evaluating alternative strategies for making loan supplies sufficient is the shape of the borrowers' demand curve. Unfortunately, nothing is known about the demand for guaranteed loans. Two illustrative demand curves have been drawn through X. D_2, a relatively inelastic demand curve, shows small reductions in the quantity of loans desired by borrowers as interest costs rise. Such a demand curve would exist if (a) the demand for college attendance and expenditures were relatively insensitive to the cost of higher education and/or if (b) there were few alternatives to guaranteed loans for financing higher education. D_1, on the other hand, is more elastic; it exhibits sharp reductions in loans demanded as interest rates rise. This situation might prevail if (a) college attendance and expenditures were highly sensitive to college costs, and/or if (b) there were many alternatives to guaranteed loans as sources of funds for students. Although some studies have attempted to estimate the responsiveness of enrollment to student charges, no one has been able to link student expenditures to loan terms.[4] Therefore, the two demand curves must be considered throughout this discussion.

To eliminate the apparent insufficiency of guaranteed student loan funds, the government has three alternatives:

1 Maintaining the cost to students at 4.25 percent while increasing the return to the lenders to R percent.

2 Encouraging the supply curve to shift to the right to pass through point L, while maintaining rates of 7 and 4.25 percent for lenders and borrowers, respectively, by changing the nonyield characteristics of loans.

3 Removing all subsidies, allowing the guaranteed loan market to clear itself.

Each of these alternatives is a "pure strategy," and combinations are possible. Pure strategies will be discussed before considering actual proposals, most of which are combinations of the above.

RAISING YIELDS TO LENDERS   The technique for raising the GLP loan volume that is most consistent with program changes in the past is to raise the yield to the lender to R. At that yield, lenders will be willing to provide the

---

[4] See, for example, Campbell & Siegel (1967, pp. 482–494). Campbell and Siegel found that college enrollments were quite unresponsive to college costs.

volume of loans *RP,* just equal to demand *X* at the subsidized interest rate. This technique suffers from two basic flaws:

1   No one knows what level of yield *R* is required. If the supply curve of lenders is very steep (as would be the case if most lenders allot fixed sums to student loans and revise the allotments only slightly as the yield varies), the required yield will be quite high. If *S* is flatter (as might be the case if lenders allowed guaranteed student loans to compete freely with other uses of funds), *R* will be only slightly above 7 percent. Recent legislation allowing a higher ceiling rate instructs the Secretary of Health, Education, and Welfare to find *R* such that:

> Whenever the Secretary of Health, Education, and Welfare determines that the limitations on interest or other conditions (or both) . . . considered in the light of the then current economic conditions and in particular the relevant money market, are impeding . . . the carrying out of the purposes . . . [of the Act] . . . and have caused the return to holders of such loans to be less than equitable . . . [he may raise the yield to the lender] (P.L. 91-95, October 22, 1969 [79 Stat. 1236]).

The inconsistency of this directive is that the yield compatible with equitableness of the return to lender is not necessarily the same as the yield required to fulfill the purpose of the act, which is to provide credit to students. Over and above that inconsistency is the overwhelming ambiguity and lack of guidance in the method the Secretary of HEW must use to discover the minimum (?) rate which does not "impede the purposes of the act."

The only permanent solution to this dilemma of casting the Secretary in the role of market forces is to supplant him by market forces. This could be done by maintaining the repayment terms to the borrower, but removing all ceilings on the return to lender. If competition prevailed, the rate *R* would be established and would "clear" the market.

2   The second objection to raising the yield to the lender, with no change in terms for borrowers, is that it is costly. A rough measure of the annual cost to the federal government for the subsidy in guaranteed loans (before yield increase) is given by the rectangle 4.25 *YZ*7. After the yield increases, annual federal costs escalate to 4.25 *XPR,* reflecting the fact that the entire burden of inducing lenders to expand loan volume is borne by the government.[5]

---

[5] It is interesting to note that a debate on the Senate floor over a bill to increase yields to lenders by up to 3 percent (over the 7 percent ceiling), which covered

Two major bills introduced in the Senate in the summer of 1969 were focused primarily on raising the yield to lenders, although neither was a pure strategy. In S. 2422, introduced by Senator Birch Bayh and 19 colleagues, the Secretary of Health, Education, and Welfare was given the power to raise yields (by up to 3 percent over the 7 percent ceiling) to lenders, but the government would pay the higher interest cost only during the enrollment and military periods. Once the repayment began, the student borrower would be required to discharge his debt at the full interest rate. For example, if the Secretary set a 2 percent premium rate for loans issued in a given period, the government would pay lenders 7 percent plus 2 percent, or 9 percent, during enrollment. The borrower's repayment schedule would be based on the full 9 percent rate established at the initiation of the loan. The effect of this procedure would be to raise the true interest cost to the borrower to about 5½ percent, equilibrating the guaranteed loan market somewhere to the left of line *XP*.[6] The net result of this procedure is to reduce the government subsidy (relative to the pure strategy of raising yields), as well as to reduce the final volume of loans.

The bill finally passed by the Congress, in the fall of 1969, the Emergency Insured Student Loan Act of 1969, as noted above, also permitted the HEW Secretary to pay a "special allowance" of up to 3 percent. However, the allowance, adjusted quarterly, is to be paid on all the *unpaid balance of the loan portfolio* of the lender for loans initiated after August 1, 1969. The meaning of this provision, which does not seem to have been generally recognized,[7] is to make guaranteed student loans into "variable interest rate" loans. That is, lenders are guaranteed a floor return

---

about 40 pages in the *Congressional Record,* never once mentioned the costs of the program. This illustrates a further bias in congressional treatment of the GLP and NDSL program: The crucial decisions on the former program are made through authorizing legislation, not through the appropriations process. The appropriation for the GLP is simply a matter of verifying the arithmetic implied by the legislative rules. See *Congressional Record* (daily ed., August 12, 1969, pp. S. 9679–9723).

[6] The discount rate required to make the present value of a 10-year stream of repayments based on a 9 percent repayment rate (starting 4 years after the loan is guaranteed) equal to the principal value of the loan is 5½ percent. See Appendix B for details of these calculations.

[7] Judged by the absence of mention in testimony by Commissioner of Education James E. Allen in the hearings on the bill (*Emergency Student Loan Act of 1969,* 1969, pp. 18–42).

of 7 percent and a ceiling of 10 percent. The actual gross return will depend on the size of the special allowance set by the Secretary of HEW over the life of the loans. By the spring of 1970, the Secretary had set the allowance at 2.25 percent (annual rate). The significance of variable-interest loans is that they provide lenders with an additional guarantee; namely, that if interest rates rise, the return on the loan will be suitably adjusted. By contrast, for most loans, and for all student loans in the past, lenders face the prospect of capital loss—a reduction in the market value of the loan paper—if interest rates rise.

The provision of some protection to lenders against rising interest rates, as embodied in the new law, ought to make guaranteed loans a more attractive investment at any given (current) interest return, particularly if lenders expect interest rates to rise. If lenders expect interest rates to fall, they might prefer loans whose returns are fixed at time of granting (as in S. 2422). Thus, the supply curve of loans may have shifted to the right with the enactment of the new provision.

SHIFTING SUPPLY CURVE As just noted, the supply curve of guaranteed loans can be shifted to the right by changing one of the nonyield characteristics of student loans, namely their ability to withstand rising interest rates. Two other techniques for increasing the supply of funds for guaranteed loans have been put forward: broadening the category of eligible lenders and creating a secondary market, for example, through "warehousing."

The list of eligible lenders under the GLP has been broadened to the point where virtually all potential sources of funds may now participate. Among eligible lenders are the 7,000 educational institutions (about half of these are vocational and foreign schools) who participate in the program, all commerical banks, mutual savings banks, insurance companies, savings and loan associations, and credit unions. By the end of fiscal year 1969, commercial banks were, by far, the largest participants, accounting for 87 percent of all loans, while thrift institutions (mutual savings banks, savings and loans, and credit unions) accounted for about 11 percent of all loans. Only 2 percent of the loan volume was contributed by the 57 lenders (out of 19,000) in the school, life insurance, and pension fund categories.[8] There would seem to

[8] Data in this paragraph from the statement of James E. Allen, August 7, 1969 (*Emergency Student Loan Act of 1969,* 1969).

be fertile ground for expanding the roster of participants in this program from the latter category. One recent proposal deserves special mention here: States may issue tax-exempt bonds and distribute the proceeds to the state university for lending to students under the GLP. Although technically the university is the lender, it is clear that the state government is playing the financial intermediary role. If states were to use this opportunity, substantial increases in lending could be expected.

It has been claimed by some students of the GLP that the lack of a secondary market for student loans has been the greatest barrier to the program's growth. In this view, the inability of lenders to convert student loan paper into cash through sale, coupled with the delayed repayment of principal for guaranteed loans, creates a liquidity crisis for lenders. Since similar problems exist for home mortgages, it is not surprising that an analogue to the Federal National Mortgage Association—which operates a secondary market for government-guaranteed mortgages —has been proposed for guaranteed loans. One version of the proposal calls for the establishment of a National Educational Warehouse Agency (NEWA) (HEW, 1969*a*).

The essence of the NEWA proposal is shown in the flow diagram outlined in Figure 4. Lenders would originate $1 million in guaranteed loans. They would receive, as in 1968–69, an interest return from the U.S. Treasury of, say, 7 percent, or $70,000. Lenders would transfer some fraction of their loan paper to the NEWA—say 80 percent.[9] For the privilege of warehousing their

FIGURE 4
Annual flow of funds under National Educational Warehouse Agency proposal, assuming loans of $1 million

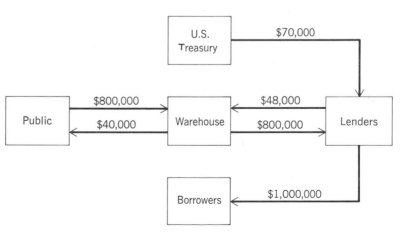

[9] Loan paper eligible for warehousing might be limited to those loans in enrollment, military, and so forth, or grace periods (see HEW, 1969*a*).

loans, the lenders receive cash for the face value of the warehoused loans and pay interest to the NEWA at the rate of, say, 6 percent, or $48,000 ($800,000 warehoused at 6 percent). The NEWA, in turn, raises its funds by borrowing from the public. Since the assets of the NEWA would consist of government-guaranteed loans, it should be able to raise capital at favorable interest rates; here it is assumed that the NEWA must pay 5 percent to its public creditors, or $40,000. The impact of the NEWA proposal is that it would provide, at no extra cost to the U.S. Treasury, a means of greatly expanding student loan activity.[10] In Figure 4, lenders would have initiated $1 million in student loans while using up only $200,000 of their own capital. The remaining $800,000 is again in the hands of the lenders, ready for relending to students or to others. Not incidentally, the provision of the secondary market by the NEWA considerably enhances the profitability of guaranteed loans to originating lenders. In the example, lenders earn $22,000 on an investment of only $200,000, making the annual return on these loans 11 percent. This rate would be obtained only as long as the loan remains warehoused. When the loan is returned to lender for collection service, the gross return falls to 7 percent. Issues of the NEWA debt would be purchased, it is argued, by many institutions (retirement funds, and so forth) that have shown reluctance to become direct participants in the GLP. Naturally, the viability of the NEWA would depend on the existence of a spread between the rate on the student loan and the interest cost of the NEWA. If the latter should rise in tight markets above the guaranteed loan rate ceiling set by statute, there can be no unsubsidized NEWA.

In March 1970, the Nixon administration introduced the Higher Education Opportunity Act of 1970 (S. 3636; 91st Cong. 2nd Sess.). Title IV, part D of the act provides for the establishment of a National Student Loan Association (NSLA), which would be a "private corporation to serve as a secondary market and warehousing facility for insured student loans." NSLA could make advances of up to 80 percent of the face amount on the security of insured loans, or it could purchase such loans outright. The prospect of warehouse advances provides lenders with a limited amount of liquidity, while the prospect of outright sale of stu-

---

[10] The NEWA would have to be chartered as a private corporation in order for its net lending to be excluded from the budget. Its $8,000 gross operating income is assumed sufficient to cover expenses.

dent-loan paper would make insured loans as liquid as other transferable assets.

In terms of this discussion of the alternative routes for expansion of guaranteed loans, the development of the NEWA or similar secondary-market institutions could be expected to produce a significant rightward shift in the supply curve for guaranteed loan funds. In Figure 3, S might shift to pass through a point such as L, with the U.S. Treasury subsidy (per dollar of loan) limited to the 1968–69 rate. Originating lenders would reap larger profits, however, as some of the providers of capital are willing to accept a lower (NEWA bond) rate of return.

The advantages of this procedure for stimulating the guaranteed student-loan market should be obvious. At no cost to the U.S. Treasury, new sources of funds would be tapped through the market-perfecting operations of the NEWA.[11] No one loses from the introduction of the NEWA (except, of course, alternative borrowers who would have obtained the capital of lenders to the NEWA). But someone gains — and herein may lie a defect of the NEWA proposal. The gross return to the originating lender may be substantially increased by the introduction of a secondary market. This gross return is not subject to a market test. Thus, NEWA may create windfall profits for initiating lenders (at present, mainly banks). This phenomenon will be treated more fully in the discussion of proposals for a National Student Loan Bank.

A FREE MARKET FOR GUARANTEED LOANS The final strategy for eliminating the apparent gap in funds for the GLP would be to remove all ceilings and subsidies in the program and convert it into a guarantee-only plan. Under this strategy, the federal government would continue to supply reserve funds to states, to reinsure state and private loans, and to offer federally insured loans. However, student-borrowers would contract for rates and repayment terms and be liable for all interest costs of the program. It is likely that competing lenders would offer plans under which borrowers could delay cash repayments until graduation, although interest would accumulate during the enrollment period. Such loans would probably bear higher charges

---

[11] NEWA perfects the market in the sense that it is willing to hold bundles of small guaranteed loans (direct securities) in exchange for issuing its own liabilities (indirect securities) that ultimate creditors are willing to purchase at lower returns than the direct securities yield.

than those involving immediate repayments, reflecting the lesser liquidity of the delayed-repayment loans.

The impact of this solution on the loan gap is difficult to predict. Depending on the nature of the demand curve of borrowers, equilibrium in guaranteed student loans will be reached at some interest rate higher than 4.25 percent and less than R. If demand is inelastic as in D_2 (in Figure 3), loan volume will exceed the amount generated under 1968–69 ceilings, but will be less than the volume discussed under the alternatives above. If D_1 is a more accurate depiction of student demand, loan volume may actually shrink below 1968–69 levels in order to equilibrate the market, reflecting the unwillingness of students to borrow when they have to bear the true cost of the loans.

This alternative cannot be evaluated without explicit consideration of the purposes and results of subsidies in the GLP, the topic of the next chapter. Clearly, unless subsidies are to be ruled out under the GLP, the conversion of the program to guarantee-only status would not represent a solution. If, however, the arguments for subsidy under this program are unacceptable, the creation of a free market in guaranteed loans would have much to recommend itself. Loans would go only to those who are willing to pay the full costs of the loan, which, in turn, represent the alternative (opportunity) uses of the funds elsewhere in the economy. Under such a free market there cannot be a question of loans being wasteful or overutilized: If borrowers are willing to pay as much as, or more than, other potential users of the funds, the reason must be that they expect a higher return (in future income, pleasure, status, and so forth) than other borrowers. Similarly, lenders cannot reap windfall profits from such a free market. Provided that lenders compete for the student dollar, excess charges will not ensue.

FUTURE CAPACITY OF THE GLP The several alternative methods for meeting the immediate crisis of guaranteed loans in 1969 have implications for the long-term prospects of this program as well. Even under the most modest loan roles envisioned in the second chapter, loan volume over the next decade will have to more than double. Unless the kinds of artificial strictures that encumbered growth of the GLP in the past are removed, there is little likelihood that it can be relied on to play a major role in loan financing. However, if the barriers are removed, and especially if new lenders are attracted through the development of secondary markets or otherwise, there is no reason to believe that financing will not be available for student loans.[12]

Table 10 provides perspective on how $1 billion in guaranteed loan volume would have affected the financial system in recent years. Guaranteed student loans are usually a part of the installment credit departments (automobiles, other consumer goods, home repair and modernization, personal loans) of commercial banks. For student loans initiated at commercial banks to have amounted to $1 billion in 1968 (as opposed to the actual level of about $400 million) would have required a very considerable expansion of the fraction of installment credit devoted to student loans: from about 10 percent to almost 25 percent. On the other hand, if banks had supplemented their student loans by diversion of funds out of other parts of their loans and securities portfolio, only 2 percent of net credit extended would have had to be diverted to reach $1 billion. The 1969 data, however, highlight the disadvantage of relying too completely on commercial banks to provide capital for student loans. In 1969, banks were selling off securities (or allowing them to mature) and investing the proceeds entirely in loans. Although installment loans seem to have fared quite well during this period, it is unlikely that stu-

TABLE 10 *Potential sources of funds for student loans, 1966–69 (billions of dollars)*	Potential source	1966	1967	1968	1969
	Net increase in installment credit at commercial banks	2.4	1.4	4.3	3.4
	*Net increase in all loans at commercial banks**	15.6	17.5	26.9	27.1
	*Net increase in all loans and securities at commercial banks**	16.1	36.6	38.9	17.1
	Net increase in assets of mutual savings banks, life insurance companies, and savings and loan associations	15.2	25.8	25.0	21.0
	Market value of endowment: 725 institutions of higher education			10.6	

*Data are for December 31, not seasonally adjusted.

SOURCES: *Federal Reserve Bulletin* (July 1970, pp. A23, A37, A38, A55), for all data except market value of endowment, which is from American Alumni Council, Council for Financial Aid to Education, and the National Association of Independent Schools (1969, p. 61). The latter data are as of the end of the academic year 1967–68.

[12] However, a special problem might arise if repayment terms were extended beyond the present 10 years. See discussion in Chapter 6.

dent loans could prosper during a prolonged or severe period of tight money. Banks expand their loan portfolios during such periods for two primary reasons:

1 To maintain good customer relations (the best customer is the large-deposit holder) and

2 To take advantage of high yields available in loans, especially installment credit (Duesenberry, 1964, Chap. 4).

Neither of these characteristics applies to guaranteed student loans, which are not likely ever, as a class, to represent good-customer loans or furnish high yields.

Thus, in the long-run, it would seem that, unless substantial amounts of capital flow into student loans from institutions other than commercial banks, the program will regularly fail during tight-money periods and will not be able to keep pace with required growth—even if loans maintain a modest role. The consequences of such a failure are the kinds of rationing systems commercial banks have used under this program in the past: servicing only the child of a customer.

It is interesting to note that in mid-1969, banks were quite open about the principles by which credit for student loans was rationed. In a letter to Senator Peter Dominick, Willis W. Alexander, president of the American Bankers Association, said:

During the past several months banks have found it necessary to ration all credit. . . . Past banking relationships provide a normal and understandable basis for such judgments. . . .

William Simmons, Jr., chief of the insured loans branch of the U.S. Office of Education, reported in Senate hearings on the subject of banks providing across-the-board assistance:

I think [there has been] in the past year, and particularly since January, more and more of what you say, this creeping in of the requirements that they be a customer, they be a good customer, they be a senior or a junior, at least they have a contract relationship for up to five years (*Congressional Record,* daily ed., August 12, 1969, pp. S. 9686–9687).

Some indication of the fiscal capacity of nonbank potential lenders is shown in the last entry of Table 10. The lack of participation in student loans by such lenders as universities and university-connected pension funds is particularly disturbing. Between academic years 1966–67 and 1967–68, the market value of total endowment at institutions of higher education increased by at least $750 million.[13] Small allocations from existing portfolios of these institutions and substantial allotments from increments to assets would have significant impact on the viability of the GLP.

---

[13] See American Alumni Council (1969, p. 63). The loan volume in the GLP in fiscal 1968 was less than two-thirds of that increase.

5. The Distribution of Benefits of Student Loans

In this chapter the questions of who should and who does benefit from student loans are explored. As noted in Chapter 1, student loan programs may serve several objectives, and it is from these objectives that some measures of the benefits of loans can be derived. Attention in this chapter is focused on discussing the goals of existing programs, estimating the distribution of their benefits, and evaluating these outcomes.[1]

ENROLLMENT EFFECTS: EQUALIZING OPPORTUNITY In testimony by federal officials before Congress, in justifications to the U.S. Bureau of the Budget, even in the smoke-filled rooms where lobbyists toil, the major benefit ascribed to existing loan programs is their ability to generate incremental enrollments. Frequently, the assumption is made that none of the borrowers under existing programs would have enrolled in college were it not for the loans they obtained. Operating for the moment under this assumption, the program results for a recent year can be examined to see whose enrollment was stimulated.

In Table 11, the first three columns report the distribution of all borrowers by the gross income of their families.[2] These distributions give some indication of the different patterns of utilization in the two programs. Fifty percent of the borrowers in the NDSL program came from families with incomes below $6,000, while only 17 percent of GLP borrowers had incomes below that

---

[1] Once again the discussion is limited to the two loan programs of the U.S. Office of Education.

[2] See Appendix C for derivation of the tables in the chapter. Gross income in the National Defense Student Loan program means "gross family income (before taxes)" as reported on the program-operating reports of the U.S. Office of Education. For the Guaranteed Loan Program, gross income means "adjusted gross income from federal tax returns," and was estimated for this study by the method set forth in Appendix C, tables C–1 to C–3.

TABLE 11 *Percentage distribution of borrowers under National Defense Student Loan and Guaranteed Loan programs by parental gross income classes, 1967–68*

Gross income class	National Defense Student Loan program borrowers	Guaranteed Loan Program borrowers	All borrowers	All borrowers as percent of students enrolled in own income class
$ 0–$2,999	22.4	8.8	15.0	62.8
$ 3,000–$5,999	27.8	8.8	17.5	24.8
$ 6,000–$7,499	16.0	10.1	12.8	18.9
$ 7,500–$8,999	13.1	10.1	11.5	16.6
$ 9,000–$11,999	13.8	22.1	18.3	17.6
$12,000–$14,999	5.0	19.9	13.1	15.1
$15,000 and over	2.0	20.3	11.9	9.8
TOTAL*	100.0	100.0	100.0	18.4

*Details may not add to total because of rounding.

SOURCES: column 1: Appendix, Table C-4, col. 3; column 2: Appendix, Table C-2; column 3: Appendix, Table C-4, col. 4; column 4: Appendix, Table C-4, cols. 1, 2, and 7.

level. By contrast, nearly two-thirds of the GLP borrowers' families had incomes above $9,000, while only one-fifth of the NDSL families had incomes so high. In the third column of Table 11, it can be seen that the median borrower's family income was about $8,000.

On the assumption that college enrollment of all borrowers is attributable to the two loan programs, the fourth column of Table 11 summarizes the effect of the programs on enrollment in each income class. According to these estimates, as much as 63 percent of the lowest income group's enrollment is attributable to the two loan programs. By contrast, only 10 percent of enrollment in the highest income category can be attributed to the joint action of both programs. In total, about 18 percent of all students on a full-time equivalency basis (FTE) "owe" their enrollment to these programs.[3]

There are two reasons why the incidence of enrollment of borrowers declines dramatically for each step up the income ladder: First, both loan programs, but especially NDSL, are

[3] To the extent that some students may have borrowed under both programs, these numbers overstate the total enrollment effects. Moreover, vocational school students are eligible to borrow under the GLP, and these borrowers are excluded from this enrollment base, so 18 percent is a high estimate, even assuming that all borrowers were induced to enroll.

generally pro-poor; and second, the base number of students is extremely small in the lowest income classes and large in the higher ones.

Thus, the incidence numbers give perhaps a too rosy picture of the two major loan programs, even accepting the assumption that all borrowers are net enrollers. In fact, very few students from lower income classes are enrolled in college, and while this situation is not the fault of the U.S. Office of Education loan programs, it provides a standard against which to measure the achievement of the loan programs. Table 12, column 1, shows how the income profile of college students would have looked if enrollment rates were the same in each income class (that is, if college students were distributed by income in the same way that families are). This is certainly an ambitious goal, but one not out of line with some of the rhetoric about equality of opportunity for higher education. Tabulated against the family-income distribution is an estimate of the distribution of college students if all student borrowers under NDSL and GLP had dropped out of school in 1967–68 (column 2 in Table 12). The actual distribution of college students is the final distribution shown (column 3). Given the assumptions, the distance between these last two distributions represents the gain in enrollment equalization attributable to loan programs, the distance between the first and second columns is a measure of the "need" for equalization. It is evident to the

TABLE 12
Percentage distribution of families, all enrollees, and enrollees assuming there are no borrowers, by parental gross income classes, 1967–68

Gross income class	Actual distribution of all families*	Distribution of enrollees assuming all borrowers dropped out	Actual distribution of all enrollees
$ 0–$2,999	10.6	2.0	4.4
$ 3,000–$5,999	23.0	12.0	13.0
$ 6,000–$7,499	13.0	12.4	12.5
$ 7,500–$8,999	11.7	12.9	12.7
$ 9,000–$11,999	16.6	19.4	19.2
$12,000–$14,999	13.1	16.6	16.0
$15,000 and over	11.9	24.7	22.4
TOTAL	100.0	100.0	100.0

*Families are defined as those with college age (18 to 24) children in 1967.

SOURCES: column 1: Appendix, Table C-4, col. 5; column 2: Appendix, Table C-4, col. 9; column 3: Appendix, Table C-4, col. 6. The percentage distribution of fall 1967 freshmen is used to estimate the distribution of total full-time equivalent enrollment.

naked eye that loan programs have made only a modest contribution toward the goals of equal enrollment rates.

Another way to see the relative weakness of the loan programs for equalization is to observe in column 1 of Table 12 that 47 percent of enrollments would have been from under-$7500-income families, had enrollment rates among income classes been equal. The third column of Table 11 indicates that only 45 percent of all borrowers are from under-$7500-income families. So, measured against the pool of potentials, existing loan programs show no equalizing tendency.

FINANCE AND SUBSIDY EFFECTS

It is, of course, not true that each borrower under existing programs represents a net enrollee in higher education. Many student borrowers would have attended college even if no federal loan programs had been available. At the opposite extreme, what are the benefits (and who gets them) if in fact *all* borrowers would have enrolled anyway?

The benefits of the NDSL and GLP under this assumption are these: (1) All borrowers are provided with an alternative (say to current family income) source of finance for their higher edu-

TABLE 13
Percentage distribution of financial benefits, 1967–68, and subsidies, 1967–69, under National Defense Student Loan and Guaranteed Loan programs, by parental gross-income classes

| | Financial benefits, 1967–68 | | |
Gross income class	Guaranteed Loan Program	National Defense Student Loan program	Total
$ 0–$2,999	8.1	n.a.†	13.1
$ 3,000–$5,999	8.1	n.a.	15.0
$ 6,000–$7,499	9.5	n.a.	11.8
$ 7,500–$8,999	9.5	n.a.	10.8
$ 9,000–$11,999	21.8	n.a.	19.0
$12,000–$14,999	20.8	n.a.	15.3
$15,000 and over	22.3	n.a.	15.1
TOTAL	100.0	100.0	100.0
Amount (millions of dollars)	435.85	236.34	672.19

* Excludes teacher-cancellation subsidies.

† Not available.

SOURCES: column 1: Appendix, Table C-3; column 3: Appendix, Table C-5, col. 9; column 4: Appendix, Table C-5, col. 10; column 5: Appendix, Table C-5, col. 12; column 6: Appendix, Table C-4, col. 6. The percentage distribution of fall, 1967, freshmen is used to estimate the distribution of total full-time equivalent enrollment. Amounts: Appendix, Table C-5.

cation costs and may therefore enroll in higher-cost schools or release funds for noneducational purposes; (2) Those borrowers who receive below-market interest rates are receiving a subsidy —a payment from the government for participating in the program.[4] Under these assumptions, the "finance benefits" and the "subsidies" can be distributed by income class of the students.

In Table 13, column 1, the distribution of benefits that derive from having been provided with a new source of finance (the GLP) are shown for fiscal year 1968. This column shows the percent distribution of the volume of loans in the GLP that year by family income class. This distribution is more skewed toward upper-income groups than the borrower distribution reported in Table 11. In 1967–68, the average loan to students from families with incomes under $3,000 was about $780, almost $200 less than the average loan in the highest income class; thus, loan volume

[4] The ultimate effects of loan programs may simply be that college charges are higher than they would otherwise be, with a resultant rise in quality or a boost in the income of the academic labor force. In the former case, the distribution of ultimate beneficiaries would look like the distribution of all college students; in the latter, the benefits would be distributed according to the incomes of the college work force—mainly faculty.

Subsidies*		Actual distribution of all enrollees
1967–68	1968–69	
13.2	14.8	4.4
15.1	17.0	13.0
11.9	12.6	12.5
10.9	11.4	12.7
19.1	18.6	19.2
15.4	13.7	16.0
14.4	12.0	22.4
100.0	100.0	100.0
183.65	211.37	

is more concentrated in higher income classes than is number of borrowers.

Unfortunately, average loan data by income class are not available for the NDSL program. In subsequent computations, the average loan is assumed to be the same in each NDSL-borrower income class.[5] Under this assumption, the total volume of GLP and NDSL loans is distributed by income class as shown in the third column of the table. Once again, greater benefits accrue to the lowest income class than would be expected if loans were distributed in accord with the distribution of the total college population (see last column of Table 13). Outside of the lowest income class, very little redistribution of financial opportunity takes place. Of 100 students, 73 are from families with incomes between $3,000 and $15,000; they get about 72 percent of the loan volume, distributed approximately in proportion to enrollment.

The distribution of subsidies granted by the two programs is only minutely more concentrated on poorer families than the financial benefits.[6] Using the subsidies implied by the 1967–68 rules of the loan programs, the distribution of subsidies is slightly more progressive (pro-poor) than the distribution of loan volume, because of the prohibition of interest subsidies in the GLP to students from families with adjusted family income of more than $15,000.[7] In 1967–68, the interest subsidy per dollar of loan in

[5] Although this assumption is not correct, there is some question about the direction of bias. In any given institution, lower-income students probably receive the largest NDSL loans, partly because these are based on need, partly because NDSL is used to match the heavily pro-poor Educational Opportunity Grants. However, poorer students tend to enroll at cheaper institutions where the average NDSL loan is smaller. This factor, taken alone, would cause a larger average NDSL for higher-income recipients. NDSL loans are by no means concentrated in low-cost, low-income institutions. In 1967–68, private institutions, which are generally higher cost and have a higher concentration of high-income students, enrolled about 33 percent of the FTE students. But they served 44 percent of the NDSL borrowers ("Percentage of Number of Students Aided," 1969; and "Percentage of Total Amount by Type of Institution," 1969) and received 48 percent of the funds. At the other extreme, two-year public colleges, with the greatest concentration of low-income students, enrolled about 15 percent of the FTE students, had 3 percent of the borrowers, and received 2 percent of the funds.

[6] In this section, the subsidy attributable to the teacher-cancellation provision of NDEA loans has been omitted.

[7] Adjusted family income of $15,000 equals $19,333 gross income, assuming a four-person family (the assumption used in the tables). Only 1.3 percent of the loan volume went to families with incomes above this level in 1967–68.

the two programs was the same—no interest during enrollment, 3 percent during repayment.

In 1968–69, two significant changes occurred in the loan programs. First, the subsidy per dollar of loan in the GLP was significantly reduced by the stipulation that students pay all interest (raised to 7 percent maximum during 1968–69) during the repayment period. Second, in 1968–69, the rate of growth in the volume of GLP loans exceeded 50 percent, while the NDSL expanded at a more modest 12 percent. These two trends have opposing implications for the distribution of subsidies: The reduction in the GLP subsidy rate increases the share of the lowest income groups in the subsidy total, while the lesser growth in the NDSL program reduces the poor's subsidy share.

The impact of these changes on the distribution of subsidies is shown in the fifth column of Table 13. The reduced subsidy in the GLP dominated the scene, and there was a small, but noticeable, shift in subsidy distribution toward the lower end of the income distribution.

The analysis of the distribution of subsidies implicit in the federal student loans programs reveals that:

- About 30 percent of the subsidies—$52 million in 1967–68 and $67 million in 1968–69—flows to students from families below $6,000 in income. This share is much higher than the incidence of such groups in the college population, but not much different from the incidence of such families in the population.

- Only about 12 to 14 percent of the subsidies—over $25 million in 1967–68 and 1968–69—flows to students from families with incomes above $15,000, well below that group's share of all college students, but not much different from that group's share of the population.

- The 60 percent of all college students whose family income lies between $6,000 and $15,000 receive about 57 percent of the subsidies: $105 million in 1967–68 and $119 million in 1968–69. There is no significant redistribution within this range: The grants could just as well have been dropped from airplanes over college campuses.

Neither assumption so far reviewed—that all borrowers are induced enrollees or that no borrowers are induced to enroll by loan programs—is likely to be true. The benefits of these programs are a mixture of enrollment and finance-subsidy effects. The mixture is dependent upon the effects of pure loans and subsidies on college attendance rates and on expenditures for higher education. In Appendix D, a model for evaluating such effects under plausible assumptions is described. Under such assumptions, the results do not differ markedly from those shown here.

EVALUATION OF SUBSIDY EFFECTS When I described the above findings to a colleague whose previous work was in evaluation of programs in the U.S. Department of Defense, his reaction was, "So, it works." When I said to him what I am going to say in the next few paragraphs, he amended his evaluation to, "Compared to Defense, it works." Fortunately, I did not report my results to any friends from the U.S. Department of Agriculture.

The distribution of potential benefits of existing loan programs has been described in this chapter. From a public-policy point of view, it is important for government decision makers to supply their own valuations as to (a) who shall be the recipients of the benefits and (b) the type of benefits.

What is the comparative value to society of a $1 benefit to a lower-income student and a $1 benefit to a higher-income student? This is not a question that allows for an answer in the form of a "proof"; it is a question of values. A strict egalitarian might argue that ameliorating the underrepresentation of students from lower-income families in higher education is *the* rationale for all student aid programs and that any benefits accruing to students from higher-income families do *not* constitute a public benefit. In other words, the enrollment (and perhaps other) gains accruing to students from families that are underrepresented (below $7,500) are the only benefits that society should value from these programs. By this reckoning, the U.S. Office of Education student loan programs are only 40 to 45 percent effective. The remaining 55 to 60 percent of the benefits are "wasted" on students to whom no public-policy weight attaches. Persons who take this position might argue for the rapid expansion of the NDSL program or other highly targeted student aid programs, such as Educational Opportunity grants, which are much more highly targeted (about 65 percent, measured by number of borrowers) on the under-$7,500 group. From this group's vantage point, a substitution of 100 NDSL borrowers for 100 GLP borrowers results in a net

increase in "worthy" borrowers of 40, so if the cost of expanding
NDSL is reducing the GLP, the favored choice is clear.

Critics of this approach to evaluating student loan programs
would point to the excessively narrow point of view expressed
by the egalitarians. Surely, the legislative history of one of these
programs, the GLP, makes clear that "middle-income students"
were intended to benefit from the programs. The GLP was supported in 1965 by the Johnson administration, in part, to head
off the more costly tax credit plans then being proposed. The
U.S. Office of Education has always defended this program as
an aid to "middle-income" youngsters. I have put quotation marks
around *middle-income* because of the variety of phenomena those
two words seem to describe to different users. The Higher Education Act proscribes interest benefits for students from families with over $15,000 adjusted family income (that is, about
$19,000 gross income for a family of four) and this is a possible
interpretation of the upper bound of "middle income." An alternative usage, one I prefer, might label the top third of all families
as "upper-income," reducing the top of the "middle-income"
range to about $10,000 gross income in 1967. However they are
defined, from the point of view that "middle-income" students
were intended to benefit, the combined effects of the two programs
might not look bad at all. The heavy targeting of NDSL takes
care of the under-$6,000-income student, while the untargeted
GLP is spread over the remaining student population (below
$15,000 gross) about as one would expect—in proportion to
enrollment in higher education. It works.

But it is here that we have to be careful to distinguish the kinds
of benefits received, as well as who gets them. One can argue
quite sensibly, I think, that what we have called "finance benefits"
—the opening up of capital markets to students—is a legitimate
and high-priority goal of the student loan programs because of
the unusual nature of human capital. Moreover, one could maintain indifference as to which income class receives such benefits,
provided that there is no evidence of lender discrimination. The
rationale for this type of aid to students is independent of their
income—it is to provide a loan to *anyone* who needs it because of
difficulty in financing highly concentrated higher education
costs out of current income.

The same argument does not hold for the *subsidy component*
in the existing loan programs. These subsidies, in the form of

zero or low interest rates, are transfer payments from the federal taxpayer to the borrower in the same way that federal welfare assistance is a transfer to eligible recipients. What is the public benefit that justifies such transfers from the taxpayer to students?

One argument might be that higher education produces social benefits not recoupable by individuals, so that general subsidies to users of higher education are necessary to stimulate private demand up to a desirable level. If this position is valid, some disturbing questions are raised. Federal loan programs now serve fewer than one-fifth of the FTE enrollment in higher education —and to a widely varying extent geographically and, probably, institutionally. What sense does it make to provide a general subsidy to higher education through such selective and capricious means?[8] Put another way, in the present state of our knowledge about social benefits, would it not be more appropriate to give such general subsidies either in the form of grants to all students or general aid to all institutions?[9] I think that the answer to this is "yes." General subsidies to higher education, to the extent they are warranted, can best achieve their purposes if they are distributed universally, through either the universe of institutions or the universe of students.[10] The choice between these modes of providing general subsidies is beyond the scope of this report. The choice between grants to students or grants to institutions involves questions of cost of administration, the

---

[8] The caprice stems from the fact that in addition to demand factors, the incidence of loans also depends on whether your father has a bank account, whether his bank has loanable funds, whether your school planned its student aid intelligently and whether it outguessed late appropriations from Congress.

[9] Until proven otherwise, it seems most neutral to assume that social benefits in the form of enlightened citizenry and leadership in politics, philosophy, and the arts would be most enlarged by broad dispersion of subsidies. The burden of proving otherwise certainly should be placed on those who advocate concentrating aid on a few.

[10] Universal loan programs—where everyone participates—are almost impossible to conceive. To achieve universality, the programs would either have to be compulsory or very heavily subsidized.

Rivlin has compared the political acceptability of compulsory loan participation to "a tax on motherhood or patriotism." See Rivlin (1961, p. 142). Encouraging total participation through large subsidies seems to me to put the cart before the horse. The level of subsidy should be determined by an evaluation of the social benefits of higher education, *not* by the requirement that everyone participate in the loan program. See the discussion in Chapter 6 on the contingent-repayment bank.

role of "consumers' sovereignty" in higher education, the issue of the role of the state, and the relation of church to state.

To summarize, existing loan programs seem to serve the objective of providing assistance to low-income students in a form that may well stimulate enrollment. This is particularly true of the National Defense Student Loan program, which is highly targeted on lower-income students.[11]

But more than half of the benefits of loan programs accrue to students from families with over $7,500 income. These benefits are partly in the form of providing access to capital markets, and a good case can be made for creating such access for all income classes. But the greater accessibility to capital markets was accompanied in 1968–69 by over $100 million in subsidies to students whose family incomes exceeded $7,500. Such subsidies cannot be defended on egalitarian grounds; they have nothing to do with capital market accessibility, and they produce inequities when viewed as forms of general subsidy to higher education.[12]

These observations apply particularly to the federal government's Guaranteed Loan Program. There is no good reason for the subsidies in that program, since the program is poorly utilized by lower-income students. Elimination of all subsidies from the GLP would, in 1968–69, have liberated about $124 million

---

[11] However, federal grant and work-study programs are even more highly targeted. NDSL should be thought of as competing with these programs for the enrollment-rate equalization objective. In 1967–68, the distribution of recipients in the Educational Opportunity Grant (EOG) and College Work-Study (CWS) programs were as follows:

Gross income class	EOG	CWS
$ 0–$3,000	28%	28%
$3,000–$5,999	40	33
$6,000–$7,499	17	16
$7,500–$9,000	10	11
$9,000 and over	5	13

SOURCE: "Distribution by Gross Family Income" (1968), based on Fiscal Year 1968 Fiscal Operations Report of number of students aided.

[12] Reminder: In this study, subsidies start when interest rates fall below the *market rate that would prevail in a "perfected" loan market* (that is, one in which risk of default to lender is nil). The difference between the laissez-faire interest rate and the perfected interest rate is *not* a subsidy as the term is used in this study. It is a measure of the capital market accessibility referred to in this section.

for grants or subsidized loans to low-income students or for general subsidies to all students (under the accounting framework of this study—not that of the federal budget). In that year, subsidies of about $30 million in the NDSL program accrued to the benefit of students with family income above $7,500.[13] These sums could as well be deployed for the purposes just mentioned.

There is nothing unique about the sins just attributed to existing federal loan programs. In attempting to achieve several objectives—stimulating enrollments of low income students, capital market accessibility, general federal subsidies for higher education—with too few (or not distinctive enough) instruments, these programs resemble other government programs which pass the political test of having something for everybody.[14] Unfortunately, this test does not produce maximally efficient programs:

- In order to give special aid to lower-income students, there probably is a role for a subsidized and targeted loan program. There is, however, no evidence that the current rate of subsidy of NDSL is adequate (or overly generous), nor has it been established that for purposes of equalization a subsidized loan is preferable to an outright grant. An even higher concentration of the funds for low-income students would clearly establish NDSL as an enrollment-equalizing program.

- There is reason for the federal government to maintain a program to provide all students with access to capital markets. This can be accomplished easily through guarantees of private loans as provided by the GLP. Since there is no good reason for the federal government to control who gets such loans, the private market (as opposed to a direct government loan) approach seems sensible. But such loans should be completely unsubsidized. Under these conditions a program such as the GLP would be a proper instrument for carrying out a public objective.

---

[13] According to Peter P. Muirhead, Associate Commissioner for Higher Education, the U.S. Office of Education intends "to limit [NDSL] loans . . . primarily to students with family incomes below $7,500 per year." (*U.S. Office of Education Appropriations for 1971,* 1970, p. 461.) If this policy is executed, it would remove most of the mal-allocated subsidies referred to here.

[14] Agricultural price supports *do* help some small, poor farms. They also may help stabilize farm production. But there are ways to accomplish each of these objectives without providing unearned subsidies to wealthy agricultural interests.

- General subsidies to higher education by the federal government may be warranted. If so, a new instrument of public policy is necessary, one which spreads the benefits more or less universally among college students. In no way do existing loan programs meet this requirement; since "willingness to borrow" is never likely to mirror "merit a public subsidy," no loan program is likely ever to be a suitable vehicle for general subsidies. There are alternative routes to general subsidy, such as general student grants, institutional grants based on enrollment, or federal support of two years of college.

6. *Proposals for Reform*

Most comprehensive studies of higher education finance have included loans for students as one component in their recommendations. Usually these programs suggest significant changes from existing loan program practice or scope. In this chapter, some of the major proposals will be reviewed and their relevance and feasibility appraised.

THE TIME-STREAM OF REPAYMENTS Present federal loan programs limit the length of the repayment term to a maximum of 10 years. There are two major criticisms of this practice, one theoretical and one practical.

To simplify matters, suppose students borrow according to a pure investment calculus; that is, they ask whether the return on the investment in education is worth the cost. If loan repayments are restricted to a period of time less than the period during which returns accrue, the investment criterion will prove stiff. The student-borrower, for example, will have to justify the costs of borrowing in terms of his first 10 years of postgraduate income, rather than by the stream of income on human capital which flows for, say, a 40-year period. To the extent that short-term repayment requirements on student loans impose this kind of penalty, while other forms of investment are not so penalized, one would expect to find relative underinvestment in higher education.[1] One way out of such a situation is to allow borrowers the privilege of continuous refinancing of loans, thus lengthening repayments into the full period over which the benefits accrue. Another way is to replace the 10-year repayment limit with a longer, but fixed, term.

The second argument for longer repayment periods grows out of the discussion in Chapter 2 of repayment ceilings. Suppose that

[1] How many toll roads would have been built if turnpike-authority bonds had been limited in terms to 10 years?

		Constant annual sum for 10 years at 7 percent	
Year After graduation	Annual income	Repayments	Percent of income
1	$ 7,000	$ 569.51	8.1
2	7,500	569.51	7.6
3	8,000	569.51	7.1
4	8,500	569.51	6.7
5	9,000	569.51	6.3
6	9,000	569.51	6.3
7	9,500	569.51	6.0
8	10,000	569.51	5.7
9	10,500	569.51	5.4
10	11,000	569.51	5.2
11	12,000		
12	12,000		
13	12,000		
14	12,000		
15	12,000		
16	12,000		
Total repayment		$5,695.10	
Average repayment rate (percent)			6.3

TABLE 14
Repayment schedules and relation to income under three student loan programs, by annual income from first to sixteenth year after graduation*

* Assumes borrower has an accumulated debt of $4,000 at graduation.
† Borrower would pay $600 and receive refund of $286.71.
SOURCE: Derived by author.

students really do think in terms of some fixed repayment ceiling, that they are unwilling to borrow beyond the point where required repayments as a percent of income in any year exceed the ceiling. Student borrowing would then be limited by the *lowest* (usually earliest) expected annual income. It makes little sense for public policy to accept this kind of limitation on student borrowing, unless the objective is to curtail severely borrowing by students. Student borrowing can be encouraged, given the constraint of a repayment ceiling, by lengthening the repayment term.

The effects of a lengthened repayment term can be illustrated by reverting to a prototypical college graduate with $9,000 average annual income. Table 14 shows the annual income of such a graduate rising from $7,000 in the first postgraduate year to $11,000 nine years later. For convenience, it is assumed that income peaks

Constant annual sum for 16 years at 7 percent		Income-proportional sum	
Repayments	Percent of income	Repayments	Percent of income
$ 423.43	6.0	$ 350.00	5.0
423.43	5.6	375.00	5.0
423.43	5.3	400.00	5.0
423.43	5.0	425.00	5.0
423.43	4.7	450.00	5.0
423.43	4.7	450.00	5.0
423.43	4.5	475.00	5.0
423.43	4.2	500.00	5.0
423.43	4.0	525.00	5.0
423.43	3.8	550.00	5.0
423.43	3.5	600.00	5.0
423.43	3.5	600.00	5.0
423.43	3.5	600.00	5.0
423.43	3.5	313.29†	2.6
423.43	3.5		
423.43	3.5		
$6,774.88		$6,613.29	
	4.2		5.0

at $12,000 in the eleventh year and thereafter. Assume that the college graduate has accumulated a $4,000 debt during his college years through borrowing in the Guaranteed Loan Program (GLP).[2] Under present arrangements, the student would sign a note committing himself to 10 annual repayments[3] of $569.51, under the 7 percent interest ceiling now in effect. Although the repayment rate

[2]   A $4,000 debt would imply $1,000 borrowed in each of four collegiate years with the government having paid interest during enrollment. If the interest subsidy (of 7 percent) were removed during enrollment and the interest cumulated to graduation, $4,000 debt would imply four annual loans of about $842. Thus, the illustration in the text can apply to an unsubsidized GLP as well as to the existing program.

[3]   In practice, loans are billed more frequently than annually. No loss in principle, and much gain in arithmetic, follow from our practice in using annual repayments.

of this debt averages about 6.3 percent of income over the life of the loan, this rate is exceeded in the first four years after graduation. If this prototype student had been sensitive to a repayment ceiling of 6 percent, he would never have accumulated a debt of $4,000; even if he had, society might not want to saddle him with burdens in excess of the ceiling.

The fourth and fifth columns of Table 14 show how a lengthening of loan terms might make a $4,000 debt "nonburdensome" to the prototype graduate. If the repayment term is extended to 16 years, constant annual payments of only $423.43 are required, and this repayment never exceeds 6 percent of income. The same result can be achieved within a 10-year repayment cycle if the interest charge is reduced to 1 percent per annum. (See Chapter 5 for a critique of interest subsidies for the GLP.) Under these extended repayment terms, the borrower pays a larger total amount for his loan, but his "burden" is reduced by financing these extra costs out of the higher incomes received in the latter years of repayment (see last two lines of table).

To the extent, therefore, that ceilings on repayments may impede students from participating in loan programs, such impediments can be overcome (in the range of debt discussed here) by lengthening repayment terms. But even the 16-year repayment term is "inefficient" in the sense that the annual repayment sum is once again determined by the lowest (first) annual income. In all years after the first, the borrower might be willing to repay somewhat more without finding repayment burdensome.

For efficiency, then, a desirable repayment scheme is one that allows maximal borrowing while keeping each annual repayment below some tolerable percentage of income. Since the annual incomes of college graduates rise over time, a repayment scheme *in which repayments are set as a percent of income* would permit borrowing of larger amounts without conflict with a repayment ceiling. The last two columns of Table 14 illustrate such a repayment scheme for the same $4,000 accumulated debt. If the borrower were required to repay exactly 5 percent of his gross income each year until the repayments discharged the loan at 7 percent interest, repayments under this scheme would continue for about 13½ years. Unlike the 10-year loan with constant annual repayments, the income-proportional repayments never exceed the 6 percent repayment ceiling. And, unlike the simple extension of repayment terms, the income-proportional method is not dependent on the size of annual income in the earliest postgraduate years. In fact, a debt larger than $4,000 could be accumulated under the income-proportional method without breaking the 6 percent of income limit.

Several recent proposals on student loan programs have taken the approach that repayment should be tied to income, or at least, that a rising schedule of repayments over time be allowed.

- *The National Student Loan Bank* Recommended by the Rivlin report, the National Student Loan Bank would provide repayment periods extending up to 30 years. "Provision would be made for rising repayments over time (in keeping with income) or constant annual payment, at the option of the borrower" (HEW, 1969c, p. 32).

- *The Percent Residual-Income Repayment Program (P.R.R.)* As described by Danière, P.R.R. would set

  the required percentage of after-tax income to be paid each year per $1,000 of aggregate loan [so that] the loan is redeemed in 10 years when income follows the expected patterns. . . . Students whose income exceeds the average will pay higher yearly amounts, and thus extinguish their loan in less than 10 years. . . . Students whose income is less than average will pay lower yearly amounts, and thus extinguish their loan in more than 10 years . . . each borrower . . . will repay fully, albeit over different time periods, at an interest which . . . is fixed at the initiation of the loan (Danière, 1969, pp. 581, 582).

- *The Carnegie Commission Bank* As originally proposed in 1968, the Carnegie Commission Bank, similar to the Educational Opportunity Bank referred to in Chapter 1, recommended a 30 to 40 year repayment term, with repayment amounts based on income. Unlike the two programs above, however, an Educational Opportunity–Carnegie Bank type of program would *not* require that *each* student retire *his* loan in full, but rather that those borrowers who prosper pay part of the costs of less successful borrowers.[4]

---

[4] However, in *Quality and Equality* (Carnegie Commission, 1970, pp. 9–13), the Carnegie Commission on Higher Education recommends a 20–30 year repayment term, with repayments of 3/4 percent of income each year for each $1,000 borrowed until the loan and accrued interest are repaid. Except for additional provision for years of low income during repayment, the revised Commission report now recommends that each student retire his loan.

Each of these plans for longer repayment terms, rising repayments over time, or repayments proportional to income can be viewed as an attempt to allow greater consumption by young college graduates at the expense of consumption in later years. In other words, using the 10-year repayment plan as a base, by moving to longer repayments or income-contingent repayments as shown in Table 14, the graduate is "borrowing again" during his first 10 postgraduate years. These borrowings bolster his ability to consume during that period. The cost to the graduate for these increased consumption expenditures in his twenties is reduced consumption expenditures in his thirties. Under the very long (30 to 40 years) repayment plans, college graduates would, in effect, be given guaranteed access to consumer loans during their twenties and thirties, to be repaid out of consumption in their forties and fifties.

Recent research into "optimum lifetime consumption" by Lester Thurow (1969a, p. 329) gives some evidence that "families desire a substantial amount of lifetime income redistribution . . . and this redistribution is heavily weighted toward the younger years of a family's life." Thurow's study contends that consumers cannot attain the desired redistribution of spending because "they cannot easily borrow for present consumption" (Thurow, 1969a, p. 324). Thus, longer repayment periods under federal loan programs involve the interplay of two kinds of capital market imperfection.

The first stems from the inability of lenders to repossess the capital acquired through education investment. An appropriate governmental response to this market failure could be the insuring, against default, of loans for educational purposes. However, a second imperfection may be the unwillingness of lenders (for whatever reason) to issue consumer loans in a volume sufficient to meet consumers' desires for intertemporal income redistribution. This additional imperfection may make the repayment term a critical determinant of whether the student borrows. By lengthening student loan repayment terms under a guaranteed or direct loan program, the government would cover the special case of the non-appropriability of educational capital, and also lower the cost of postgraduate consumer loans to the loan-program participant.

Thurow's findings help in evaluating proposals for lengthening the terms on student loans. First, provision for government-supported guarantee programs with lengthy repayments clearly raises an equity issue. Why should better access to consumer loans be limited to college graduates or participants in an education bank? If the case can be made for allowing greater consumption for young families, the case is at least as strong for non–college-goers (who have fewer alternatives) as for college graduates. The public benefits of equalized enrollment rates would have to pay for this "inequity" effect.

Second, extending the term of national defense student loans not only would give graduates access to consumption loans, but would allow such access at highly subsidized interest rates. Although subsidies may be warranted for an explicitly equalizing NDSL program, extension of the subsidy into the future seems to carry things a bit too far. There is no evidence that guaranteed access to low-interest consumer loans would stimulate enrollment or that it is fair to favor people in their twenties who attended college over those who did not.

Third, the GLP, with all subsidies removed, might be an appropriate place to allow lengthened terms or arrangements to make repayments rise with income. Moreover, the GLP under these circumstances might be made accessible to all young persons, thus converting it into a "young people's loan program" designed to serve as a general vehicle for intertemporal redistribution of consumption. The program could offer annual loans up to some maximum amount to all young people and provide them with long-term repayments (either fixed term or variable term as in Danière's proposal) increasing with age (either fixed schedule or one contingent upon income). This proposal is one step beyond that of James Tobin in "Raising the Incomes of the Poor" (Gordon, 1968, pp. 91–92). Tobin suggests that an endowment of $5,000 be made available to every person on graduation from high school or age nineteen. The endowment could be drawn upon for expenses or subsistence, for higher education, vocational training, apprenticeship, or on-the-job training. Repayments would be through an income tax surcharge after the age of twenty-eight. Tobin's rationale is to give a young person "the opportunity to develop his capacity to earn income and to contribute to the society."[5]

The right question to ask about lengthened repayment arrangements has very little to do with higher education as such. It is

---

[5] I fail to see how the permissible activities that Tobin lists are to be distinguished from "a visit to Europe," "spending a year tutoring poor kids," "feeding my baby better so that he will not be sick when I decide to work again" — or any other purpose — even on Tobin's "capacity to earn" grounds.

whether society is willing to redistribute consumption (and investment) opportunities toward younger persons and away from other claimants on the national output. Even though the program is unsubsidized, as set forth here, the purchasing power of younger persons would be enhanced, and this increased command over resources would have to be offset elsewhere in the economy. Private investment could be curtailed through higher interest rates or corporate taxes, or consumption by the nonyoung could be reduced through increased individual income taxes. Public expenditures could be reduced (Shell et al., 1968, pp. 33 ff.). The question is whether these reductions are worth the enhancement of consumption and investment by younger persons. It would be nice to reduce these gains and losses to a simple formula. But it can't be done. Even if, in the very long run, everyone were agreed that society would be better off with a lifetime pattern of purchasing power more heavily concentrated on the young, and even if society could agree that the enhanced productivity engendered by greater postsecondary investment is worthwhile, there would be costs during the transition. During that transition period, the nation would have to give up something to provide resources for the young. And the diversion of such resources are real costs to those who have to bear them. There is no free lunch.

To summarize the discussion of lengthened and/or income-related repayments: Lengthening repayments under the NDSL program would provide a *subsidized* access to greater consumption for young college graduates who have borrowed under that program. In general, there is no good reason to ask society to pay for consumption by college graduates. If lengthening the repayment period is intended to enhance the enrollment equalizing and generating effect of NDSL, there ought to be evidence that this particular form of subsidy is more effective than others. To my knowledge, there is no such evidence. On the other hand, it seems unobjectionable to encourage colleges to offer, within the 10-year repayment term and within the present subsidy, repayment schedules that rise within the 10-year period. Most schools participating in the NDSL program do allow such repayment arrangements, but discourage their use. The reason for this is intimately tied to teacher cancellations, to be discussed later in this chapter.

A case can be made for lengthened and/or income-contingent repayments in an *unsubsidized* program. The case is based on the general failure of capital markets to allow young people to enhance their purchasing power at the expense of expenditures later in life. It is argued here that such a privilege should not be limited to young persons who attend college, but should be open to all. Unless it can be demonstrated that people who do not go to college do not want to reallocate their lifetime expenditures while college-goers do, the appropriate public policy would be an unsubsidized loan program with lengthened repayments open to all young people. Such a program in its early years, at least, would require the non-young to defer their command over current resources to make them available to youthful borrowers.

NATIONAL STUDENT LOAN BANK Thus far the discussion has ignored institutional impediments to lengthened and income-contingent repayments. Even without such changes in existing student loan programs, there may be some reason for establishing a centrally administered loan bank. But lengthier loans and income-contingent plans would make a National Student Loan Bank essential.

- If loan repayment amounts were made contingent upon income, the collecting agency would need access to the borrowers' tax reports. It is not likely that such access could be, or should be, provided to lenders under either the NDSL or GLP programs as presently administered.

- Lengthened repayment terms would exacerbate the difficulties already present in attracting loan funds to the GLP as it presently operates. A longer repayment term would make student loans appear even less liquid to banks, and collection costs to the lender would escalate as families move during the years. Under these circumstances, the financing of a large-scale loan program would have to move beyond the narrow confines of commercial-bank finance presently occupied by the GLP.

Although there have been several major proposals for a centralized facility for loans to students in higher education, few institutional details have ever been provided. One exception is a bill introduced by Senator Walter F. Mondale and 18 other senators in April, 1969. Title III of the Mondale bill, S. 1788, provides for a "Higher Education Loan Bank," which would "not be an agency or instrumentality of the United States Government." (The intent of this provision is to keep the activities of the Bank out of the federal budget.) The Bank would make loans to students for a period of up to 30 years at deferral and interest terms similar to those under the GLP. It would be "authorized to utilize the services of financial institutions and postsecondary or higher education institutions in the initiation of loans and . . . pay reasonable compensation . . . for services rendered." The Bank could "enter into agreements with the . . . Internal Revenue Service" to collect principal and interest on loans. The Higher Education Loan Bank would raise funds (up to $5 billion outstanding at any one time) by issuing its own obligations which would be guaranteed against default by "the full faith and credit of the United States" (Student Assistance Act of 1969, April 14, 1969, pp. 33–45).

To provide an understanding of how such a Bank would work and how it differs from the secondary-market proposal reviewed in Chapter 4, a flow diagram for the Higher Education Loan Bank has been constructed.

Figure 5 shows the Bank raising $1 million from "the public" (individuals and institutions) and paying interest of $50,000 on its obligations (5 percent annual rate).[6] The Bank lends the $1 million to students, and, during the enrollment period, it collects 7 percent interest from the U.S. Treasury. The Bank compensates loan initiators (college and financial institutions) by some indeterminate sum for originating loans.

How does this proposal differ from the pure secondary-market operation described previously? The differences can be discussed under three headings representing functions in the student loan market: acquisition of capital, origination of loans, and collection of repayments.

Acquisition of Capital Under a central loan bank, all the necessary capital is raised from the public directly through the issue of federally backed obligations of the bank. Under the GLP cum secondary market, part of the funds are raised centrally through bonds of the secondary-market institution, the remainder by lending institutions. Since a federally backed institution clearly would have lower borrowing costs than individual lenders, and would be more able to vary the nature of its debt obligations (for example, as to size and term) than individual lenders, total borrowing costs would be minimized as there is

---

[6] In the National Warehouse proposal reviewed in Chapter 4, it was assumed that the NEWA could borrow at 5 percent. The Higher Education Loan Bank should have borrowing costs very close to borrowing costs of the U.S. Treasury if its obligations are guaranteed by the United States government.

FIGURE 5
*Flow diagram
for the loan
stream of a
Higher Education
Loan Bank*

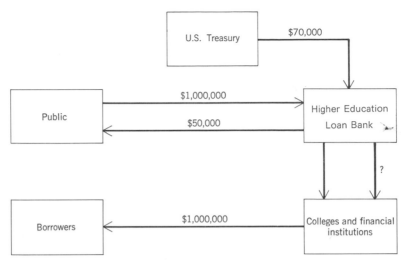

greater reliance on central finance. Thus, only if the secondary institution raised almost all of the funds under the GLP would total borrowing costs be minimized. If such a practice were followed under the National Educational Warehouse proposal, the entire spread between the Warehouse's borrowing costs and the interest rate paid by the U.S. Treasury *might accrue to originating lenders.* Under the Higher Education Loan Bank, this spread *would accrue to the national bank itself.*

Origination of Loans

Under the Higher Education Loan Bank, student loans are originated either by the national bank itself or by colleges or financial institutions acting, for a fee, as agents of the Bank. In the GLP, loans are originated by any eligible lender who is willing to commit capital to the program. For the most part, originating lenders have been commercial banks. The institution of a secondary market of the National Educational Warehouse Agency type would mean that costs of originating loans would have to be met by originating lenders out of the spread between the student borrower's interest rate and the rate the Warehouse charged banks for warehousing loan paper. Unless that interest charge were regulated so as to provide just enough income to meet originating costs, the possibility exists for windfall gains to originating lenders. Under the Higher Education Loan Bank, the central institution, as the legislation is written, could originate loans by itself or contract out the responsibility, or, in principle, put the fees for loan-origination up for bid. The essential difference here is that the Higher Education Loan Bank could use a variety of "vendors" with some hope of limiting fees to actual costs. A warehouse agency could perform a similar function if it placed its own capital at the disposal of colleges for purposes of lending to students and then paid the college a fee for placement.

Collection Under the GLP cum Warehouse, the collection of repayment is the responsibility of the originating lender. Any costs of collection are met out of the total interest income received by the lender. Under the Student Assistance Act of 1969, collection costs are not very well spelled out. Although the Higher Education Loan Bank may make arrangements with the U.S. Internal Revenue Service to collect, it is not clear whether such services would be paid for by fees from the Bank or out of congressional appropriations to IRS. The principal difference between the Higher Education Loan Bank and the secondary-institution scheme is the introduction of IRS as the collection agency in the former proposal.

Evaluation The institution of a national bank to provide loans to students seems superior in many respects to amending the GLP with a federally chartered secondary institution. To the extent that a secondary market has the virtue of attracting new sources of funds to student loans, the national bank capitalizes on this virtue. Commercial banks could participate in the national bank by buying its obligations. And so could other financial institutions—and even colleges and universities. The national bank's lesser reliance on commercial banks also means that the vicissitudes of monetary policy may be less strongly felt in the student loan market and that, in any event, student loans would be placed in less direct competition with auto and house repair loans, whose relation to higher education is purely a product of bank organization. On the other hand, despite its off-the-budget charter, a national bank would be a federally sponsored organization absorbing large amounts of capital.

The procedures for origination of loans under a national bank seem also quite advantageous. The national bank is free to contract with commercial banks, for a fee, to initiate student loans. To the extent that commercial banks are actually chosen for this function under a national bank, the only difference from present procedures would be that explicit charges for origination would be made, rather than hidden in total program costs. My guess, however, is that the banks would play almost no role in the initiation of student loans under a national bank, and that colleges would originate most loans. The reason for this is simple: There is no aspect of the process of originating student loans at present for which banks have any comparative advantage. Loan applications under the GLP now contain three principal components: (1) a statement of other financial aid received by the applicant, (2) a statement of tuition and other educational costs, and (3) a statement of family income. The first and second components are at present verified by, or completed by, the educational institution. The last component is completed by the student and his parents, who sign a sworn statement allowing the U.S. Commission of Education to obtain a copy of the family's federal income tax return. The commercial bank's function, therefore, in initiating loans, is simply to review data that are already verified or that are unobtainable by the bank. On the basis of the review, the bank establishes whether the applicant is eligible for the federal interest subsidy (which can be accomplished by a computer—the only question is whether line 30G on the federal loan form exceeds $15,000) and decides whether to lend.[7] At this decision point, commercial loan criteria have been applied in the past, and in a manner prejudicial to lower-income students. This practice has been mentioned in the Chapter 5 discussion of the GLP.

Thus, even under present rules, banks are not particularly well-suited to initiate student loans. If the GLP were altered along lines discussed previously—eliminating all subsidies in GLP and broadening it to include all young people—banks would be no better suited to initiate loans. Indeed, under such a broadened program, initiating a loan would involve little more than verification of a social security number and the dispensation of funds, activities which could most simply be performed by the U.S. Social Security Administration, which would be a natural contract agency for dispensing youth loans under a national bank.

When we turn to the collection function, answers are, in a way, too easy. If repayments are to be contingent on income, the IRS is the most sensible collector. Even if repayments were to be set on a fixed (constant annual or rising) schedule, a good case can be made for IRS doing the job of collecting repayments. A large share

---

[7] On the Student Application for Federally Insured Loan, line 30G is "adjusted family income."

of the cost of both the NDSL and GLP has been for collection. Frequent billings, in small sums, to a geographically mobile population over a 10-year period, are a collector's nightmare. If loan terms were extended, the collection problem would become worse. Only the IRS could collect this type of loan with minimal marginal costs.[8]

It would be imprudent to drop this discussion of collections here. At least from the point of view of the U.S. Treasury, the use of IRS for collecting student loans is a radical proposal and second-best solutions are in order. Barring IRS collections, a good case can be made for commercial banks as repayment collectors. There is some evidence that they are superior to colleges and universities for this purpose. Some colleges now use banks to perform collection services (*Notes and Working Papers*, 1968, p. 40). The record of the commercial banking sector's ability to handle loan collections under the GLP is, as yet, undetermined but seems destined to be better than that of NDSL institutional participants.

The establishment of a national loan bank need not preclude the use of commercial banks as collection agencies. Appropriate wording could be written into enabling legislation to allow the national bank to contract with banks (or insurance companies or state agencies) for collection services. The important advantage of a national loan bank is, once again, that it allows separation of function and fee-for-service, rather than the inappropriate reliance on commercial banks that the GLP-NEWA proposal implies.

A national loan bank incorporating the features discussed above is feasible. It could operate without subsidy, set rates to borrowers to meet costs of raising capital, and provide collection and origination services. Such a bank could offer long-term repayment schedules and, with IRS cooperation, make annual repayments contingent upon income. Eligible borrowers could include young people not presently eligible for guaranteed loans.

A national bank could serve as the dispensing agent for a subsidized NDSL program as well. Congress would appropriate annual interest subsidies to the national bank, which would then borrow

---

[8] Among the myriad possibilities for tying IRS to the GLP, without establishing a national bank, would be an arrangement whereby the student borrower signed parallel contracts with the originating lender and a special federal agency. The agency would make the loan repayments to the originating lenders (saving collection costs because of single billings) and would also arrange with IRS to collect repayments from the borrowers, perhaps at more extended terms than in the original contract.

from the public, using low interest student repayments and Congressional appropriations to repay its borrowings. The national bank could offer NDSL borrowers (a) 10-year repayments at low interest rates *or* (b) longer-term repayments (with or without income-contingent annual repayments) at full interest costs. Such an option is not likely to produce worse enrollment results than the present system, inasmuch as option "a" *is* the present system.

The NDSL program could be articulated in another way, more in keeping with the separation of guarantee versus subsidy activities. The national loan bank could be made *the exclusive* loan program. Low-income students would be treated like all other borrowers as far as the bank is concerned. (This discussion ignores teacher cancellation provisions of NDSL.) However, any borrower whose family income falls below the low-income cutoff point would be eligible for a grant from the U.S. Office of Education equivalent in size to the implicit subsidy in the NDSL program. The student could use the grant to reduce his future repayments (in which case the loan is identical to the present NDSL program) or to supplement his current enrollment costs. This procedure would allow students to make the judgment as to when the federal subsidy is to be realized, rather than the (uninformed) centralized decision that is now implicit in the NDSL program.

To illustrate how the national bank might work with a "subsidy division," assume an unsubsidized freshman enters college in the fall of 1971. In the summer of 1971, he obtains a loan of $762.90. By the summer of 1975, when he graduates, the loan of $762.90 will have accumulated interest (at 7 percent, assumed bank rate) so as to result in a $1,000 debt. With a 10-year repayment term commencing in the summer of 1976, the borrower will have to repay $142.38 annually until 1985 for his freshman loan.

Now let us take a low-income student entering college in the fall of 1971. He also borrows $762.90. Under the current NDSL rules, such a student, assuming he does not drop out, would repay his debt between 1976 and 1985 at the rate of $89.44 per annum. This sum is the annual repayment on a $762.90 loan repaid over 10 years at 3 percent. As discussed previously, and as this illustration should make clear, the NDSL student's subsidy consists of the $52.94 ($142.38 minus $89.44) reduction in annual repayments, from 1976 to 1985, that the NDSL provisions allow. (The $52.94 reflects both the absence of interest accrued during 1970–1974 and the low interest during repayment.) The present value, as of summer 1971, of ten "gifts" of $52.94 received from 1976 to 1986, discounted at 7 percent, is $283.66. This total represents the true cost to the federal government of the NDSL.

The recommendation made above is that the low-income student borrow from the national bank in exactly the same way as the unsubsidized student, but that he receive a check for $283.66 in the summer of 1971. If he deposits the check with the national bank, the bank will reduce payments to $89.44, the net result being identical, from the student's point of view, to an NDSL loan. The student may, however, use the $283.66 for current costs, in which case he must repay his loan at the full $142.38 annual rate. This added option involves no greater federal subsidy than is now present in the NDSL program. Moreover, as indicated before, the net effect on the federal budget of incorporating NDSL operations into a national bank *under present budget accounting rules* would be a substantial reduction in budget costs.

This illustration ignores details of management and fine points of the plan, all of which seem manageable.[9]

The effect on the federal budget of integrating the NDSL program into the national bank would be a substantial reduction in apparent costs of the program. The federal capital contribution (about 70 percent of loan volume) would be removed from the federal budget. In its place would go the annual implicit subsidy (about 30 percent of annual loan volume), resulting in a "budget saving" of about $100 million at fiscal 1969 levels. ("Budget savings" would be even greater if repayments on past loans were returned to the U.S. Treasury.) A shift of this type would restore some semblance of balance between the NDSL and GLP budget treatments.

A major issue for a national loan bank with a subsidy operation would be whether to allot loan funds to institutions, as is presently the case under the NDSL program, or whether to deal directly with the borrower. In permitting college financial-aid officers to "package" grants, loans, and employment funds for students, institutional allotments are alleged to be more effective in attracting low-income students. To my knowledge this proposition has never been tested. We do not know whether the availability of portable-loan aid for lower-income students—and

[9] An example of legislation incorporating many of the features described in the above discussion is H. R. 16621, The Higher Education Opportunity Act of 1970 (Title IV, part B).

commensurate reduction in the fraction of college-dispensed aid to be "packaged"—would, in fact, lower enrollment rates for low-income students. A national bank operating a subsidy division could experiment with alternative institutional arrangements to find those which lead to the greatest increase of enrollments by low-income students. For example, the bank might experiment with freshmen by dividing the nation into three blocs of states. In one bloc, the bank would deal directly with students, making advance loan commitments to high school seniors. In another bloc, it could allot commitments to college-aid officers in accordance with present procedures. And in the third sector, the bank might try allocating commitments to high school systems, appealing to them to locate and guide their disadvantaged youth toward college. If the subsidy division of the national bank adopts normal bureaucratic behavioral rules ("growth of program measures success"), there would be ample incentive for the bank to shift toward the allotment procedure that is most suited to the goal of attracting low-income students.

To summarize, a national loan bank could provide the means to attract new capital into student loans. It could perform the critical functions of lending—origination and collection—efficiently under a flexible charter. It could make repayment terms more flexible and responsive to income. A bank could also funnel the subsidy elements in present loan programs, at a saving to the federal budget, with some prospect that new techniques of allotment could further the goals of present subsidies.

One further potential advantage of a national loan bank derives from the possibility that the United States may be entering a historical phase of "capital shortage" perhaps combined with secular price inflation. This possibility stems from projected demographic and other trends, which imply historically low private savings rates and historically high demands for capital by business and governments in coming decades.[10] If this prognosis is true, then 1969 may be but the first taste of a long-term trend in the economy. One characteristic of the 1969 experience, commented on at length in the financial press, may be particularly relevant for student loan program prospects. I refer here to the "straight debt is dead" argument.[11]

[10] For a discussion of these trends, see Kuznets (1961, especially chap. 10).

[11] See, for example, "Not Enough Money To Go Around" (1969, pp. 167–170).

It is possible that in an era of general capital shortage and price inflation, lenders will be unwilling to commit long-term funds for conventional debt issues. In the corporate sector, this implies a growing reliance on convertible debt or other securities that offer lenders an "equity kicker," ensuring that the provider of capital will share in the real or price-induced gain his provision of capital makes possible. If lenders in coming decades insist on such forms of securities, it is clear that fixed-interest student loans will not be able to compete effectively in capital markets.

A conceivable plan for providing an "equity kicker" to suppliers of student loan capital is suggested by the Swedish Study Funds System. Without getting into all the details, reliance in the Swedish system on loans that are inflation-proof is relevant here.[12] Swedish students in higher education receive state study funds that are linked to base amounts of the national supplementary pension, which is adjusted for price changes. The student commits himself to repay a portion of the study funds advanced in *terms of units of the national supplementary pension at the time of repayment.* If the cost of living, and thus the national pension, in Sweden should rise over a borrower's repayment cycle, his nominal "dollar" repayments will be larger. In effect, the student commits himself to repay in terms of real (price-corrected) money.

The connection between the Swedish system and a national loan bank is that the bank could issue loans to students with repayments to be made in price-corrected dollars. In so doing, the bank could issue to *its* creditors fixed-purchasing-power bonds. These bonds would tie both principal and interest to some index of the price level, presumably the consumer price index. As Tobin points out, such bonds would fill a gap in the current menu of alternatives available to savers—the gap consists of the nonavailability of savings instruments that protect the holder against price inflation without increasing his risk of non–price related changes in rates of return—and would, thus, compete favorably with both equities and conventional bonds (Tobin, 1963, pp. 202–210). By operating a national bank on both the receipts and expenditures side on an "escalator basis," such an institution could overcome a general market movement against conventional debt.

A national bank could move to the extreme in competing for

[12] These details are summarized in Swedish Institute for Cultural Relations with Foreign Countries, (1968).

equity finance by issuing debt whose repayment is tied not only to price-level changes but also to productivity advances in the economy. Such a plan could, for example, tie bond repayments to a wage or family-earnings index.[13] Here creditors would be buying shares in a mutual fund of labor income. The obvious complement to such a national bank security would be for the bank to base its charges to borrowers *on wage incomes.* Thus, borrowers would borrow in terms of current wage-units and would contract to repay their loans in terms of future productivity-and-price enhanced wage units. One would expect college graduate incomes to move in line with any general wage index. Such a method of financing student loans comes 90 percent of the way to the Educational Opportunity Bank, the next topic for discussion. However, it should be pointed out that in none of the income-contingent repayment plans has the possibility of issuing productivity-and-price sensitive bonds been advocated. This perhaps stems from the fact that most writers in this field have focused on student borrowers and their needs and very little on the attractiveness of alternative offers to suppliers of capital.[14]

To the extent that one views the prospects for nonequity finance as pessimistically as the above discussion presupposes, the advantages of a national loan bank are evident. Individual lenders are unlikely in the extreme to be willing to issue price- or productivity-adjusted debt to attract borrowers. In any event, a National Student Loan Bank could retain the future option of using the finance methods just outlined, even if it does not initially do so.

The loans given by the national bank described in this section are all similar in requiring students who obtain loans to repay in full.[15] Even the subsidized student is given a fixed schedule

[13] A similar program of adjustments has been proposed for social security benefits. For a discussion, see Pechman, Aaron, & Taussig (1968, pp. 98–104).

[14] One writer has considered equity finance for students. William Vickrey suggested that capital suppliers share in the productivity of the cohort to whom the capital is advanced. Under his proposal, the lending agency would set repayment rates at a fairly high level. Then, if the incomes of the borrowing cohort prove high enough, any surplus earned by the lending agency would be shared "one-third for the account of investors and two-thirds . . . for the payment of retirement benefits" to the borrowers. See Vickrey (1962, p. 277).

[15] Defaults due to death, disability, and the like have not been discussed here. A national bank can sensibly handle cases of default by imposing a small insurance charge on each loan.

of (lower) repayments to meet. In the case in which annual repayments are contingent upon income, each borrower will eventually repay his loans, although the period of repayment may vary. It is this contractual quality of loans that distinguishes the national bank described here from the Educational Opportunity Bank supported by the Zacharias panel (HEW, 1969c, pp. 63–65) and the Carnegie Commission report of December 1968 referred to previously. The Educational Opportunity Bank builds upon the features described above, and additionally attempts to mutualize the risk of investing in higher education. Risk of earning low incomes is collectively borne by a year's cohort of borrowers; even though *the cohort must repay its loans, each member of the cohort need not repay his loan.* Since repayments to the Educational Opportunity Bank are based on income, former students whose incomes are low relative to their borrowing will be subsidized by other former students whose incomes are high relative to their borrowings. It should be immediately evident that such an arrangement has the potential for attracting to the Bank only those who, for whatever reason, anticipate low earnings. This "adverse selection" of Educational Opportunity Bank participants has been addressed and allegedly countered by the study of the proposal by Karl Shell and others. (Shell et al., 1968). In the next section, their attempt to randomize the participation in the Bank is reviewed.[16]

THE EDUCA-TIONAL OPPOR-TUNITY BANK In an analysis of the Educational Opportunity Bank proposed by the Zacharias panel, Karl Shell and colleagues (1968, pp. 2–45) present estimates of the tax rate required to make such a Bank self-sustaining. Much to the surprise of some observers, and at some variance with other studies, the required tax rate for educational borrowing is quite low in all of Shell's alternative models: around 0.3 or 0.4 of 1 percent per \$1,000 of debt, never in excess of 1 percent. For a debt of \$12,000 accumulated during college,

[16] Vickrey attempts to deal with adverse selection by having the lending agency "rate" student borrowers by earnings potential as determined by grades, tests, and so forth. "Adverse selection would thus be limited to cases in which the student has a genuinely better basis for the appraisal of his prospects than that provided by the rating" (Vickrey, 1962, p. 276). In my view, the educational consequences of this proposal are exceeded only by its political infeasibility. (The rating system implies that for any given future income level, the marginal rate of tax on that income level will be lower, the "smarter" the student is.)

these tax rates imply repayment rates of only from 4 to 5 percent of income. In a similar study of a tax-based college finance plan for England, repayment estimates were on the order of from 10 to 25 percent of income. (Glennerster, Merrett, & Wilson, 1968). In this section the Shell article will be reviewed, simplified into a form amenable to primitive arithmetic, and then some of the results challenged.

The Shell Bank allows students to borrow for their college education by committing themselves to the repayment of τ percent of income per $1,000 borrowed for terms of from 30 to 40 years. Since a plan with only this provision would be likely to lead to adverse selection of participants—that is, only people with low-income prospects would join—Shell specifies an "opt-out" rate. Under this provision, the Bank would set an opt-out rate R, such that if the borrower's repayment stream at any point is equivalent to the full amortization on a conventional loan of R percent, he will be excused from further repayments. For example, suppose a student has borrowed $1,000 and the opt-out interest rate is 8 percent. The tax rate is, say, 1 percent of income. If, one year after the loan is granted, the student earns $108,000, he will pay a tax of $1,080. Such a payment exactly requites the $1,000 loan at 8 percent interest. The borrower never again has to pay the Bank. Borrowers may, of course, opt-out voluntarily at any time at interest rate R. The effect of this provision is to place a ceiling on the true interest cost to the borrower in the Bank. No one pays more than R percent interest.

Given certain plausible assumptions about the growth of income of men and women college graduates (and a set of alternative rules for the taxation of married women), about who will borrow how much, and about who marries whom, the key variables in the Educational Opportunity Bank are related as follows:

$$\tau = f(r,R)$$
$$+\;-$$

(1)

where τ is the tax rate (percent of income) per $1,000 borrowed, R is the opt-out interest rate, and r is the rate of return of the Bank.

The rate of return of the Bank (r) represents the annual interest rate the Bank would be able to pay its creditors if the Bank were self-financing. It is, in effect, the gross profit rate (for any cohort of borrowers) of a bank that sets an opt-out rate of R and a tax-rate of τ per $1,000.

The signs under the equation represent the signs of the partial derivatives of the variables. Given the rate of return of the Bank, the higher R is, the smaller the necessary τ is. This is because as R is increased, given the future income of borrowers, more people will be "opting-out" at a higher repayment rate than before R was increased. The higher profits gleaned from these higher-income borrowers allow the Bank to lower charges to all other borrowers. A higher R creates a larger surplus (earnings of the Bank above r) to be used to subsidize borrowers with below-average earnings.

On the other hand, given R, an increase in r raises the required tax rate. *Given the income of Bank participants,* an increase in the required earnings of the Bank *(r)* can only be achieved if R is raised (ruled out by assumption here) or if τ is raised.

The relationship between r, R, and τ is illustrated by Shell in the diagram reproduced as Figure 6.

The curve in Figure 6 shows all combinations of τ and r that result from the assumed future income, and so forth, of borrowers

FIGURE 6
Rate of return as a function of the repayment tax rate (τ) for student borrowers entering college in 1969*

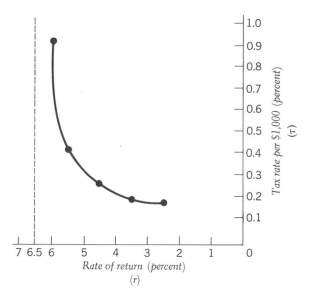

Rate of return *(percent)*
(r)

Tax rate per $1,000 *(percent)*
(τ)

*Assumptions: repayment period set at 40 years; annual growth rate of income of borrowers, 4.5 percent; opt-out interest rate R, 6.5 percent.

SOURCE: Shell et al. (1968, p. 22).

of the Bank. The conclusion drawn from this relationship by Shell and colleagues (1968, p. 22), is:

. . . in a well designed program, the opt-out interest rate R should be set substantially higher than the rate of return r. As r approaches R, the repayment-tax rate τ becomes very large. With τ high, participants in the program will have to make large repayments in the years immediately following college graduation.

It might also be pointed out that a high τ might induce work disincentives and, perhaps most important, it might make the Bank politically unsellable.

In all the calculations of alternative models presented in the Educational Opportunity Bank paper, the dictum above is scrupulously obeyed: R is always set at least 1.5 percentage points above r.[17] The selection of such a wide gap between R and r is critical to keeping the calculated τ as low as it is in the Shell paper, as can be seen on the diagram.

A positive rate of subsidization s of the Bank (that is, the difference between the cost of funds i to the Bank and the rate of return r of the Bank) is justified according to Shell "on the ground that there are benefits which accrue to the society as a whole from college education, but which are not measured by increased income to the educated person" (Shell et al., 1968, p. 10). Although no one claims to know just how big these benefits are relative to purely private benefits, the Bank, or Congress in enabling legislation, would establish a subsidy rate that seemed to meet the requirements.

The operation of the Shell Bank can now be shown as a system of equations determining all the key variables as follows:

$$\tau = f(r,R) \tag{1}$$
$$R = r + k \tag{2}$$
$$r = i - s \tag{3}$$

Equation 1 is a repetition of equation 1 preceding. Equation 2 expresses the need "in a well-designed program," to keep R substantially above r: k is positive and large. Equation 3 indicates that the rate of return r of the Bank may be set below the cost of funds i by s percentage points, where s is determined by the degree

---

[17] With one exception, which is used in the discussion immediately following.

of social benefits produced by education. *s* is the subsidy measured in percentage points.

A Bank manager might use these equations as follows. First, it is necessary to look to the market to establish *i*, the cost of funds to the Bank. Then *s* must be subtracted from *i* to get *r* (equation 3). Once *r* is known, *R* may be selected such that τ is kept quite low (that is, use equation 2 with a reasonably large *k* to find *R*). With *r* and *R* established, τ can be found from equation 1 by computing the tax revenues to be paid by college graduates.

This plan would work well if all college students (or a representative sample of them) in fact joined the Bank. But the distribution of participants may not be independent of the levels of the variables in the system. Indeed, the opt-out interest rate was invented to avert nonparticipation of students who anticipated high incomes. Taking into account the fact that participation and the terms of the Bank's loans are interrelated, it is far less certain that τ can be held down and that *s* can be limited by exogenous considerations. This can be demonstrated as follows:

Rewrite equation 1 as:

$$\tau = f(r,R,Y)$$
$$+-- \tag{1a}$$

where *Y* is the average income of Bank participants.

Since participation in the Bank will vary, it is necessary to take into account the possibility that the earnings level of participants will also vary. For simplicity, consider all students as coming from two discrete groups: those expecting low incomes and those expecting high incomes. Suppose further that *on average* these expectations are correct—the future income of the second group will exceed that of the first group. Equation 1a indicates that the τ set by the Bank will depend on the mix of the two expectations groups among Bank participants. Specifically, if the Bank attracts a small proportion of high-income expecters, the average *Y* of the Bank will fall and, all else equal, τ will have to be higher than in the previous assumptions. In the Shell Bank, *Y* was fixed and assumed to be at the mean for various demographic and economic categories in the college graduate population.

We now hypothesize that the average income of Bank participants is given by

$$Y = g(R - i)$$
$$- +$$

(4)

where $(R - i)$ is the price that Bank participants pay for insurance against too burdensome a debt; it is the "insurance premium" of the Bank. The market interest rate i is what a borrower would have to pay for a conventional (guaranteed) loan; the opt-out rate R is the maximum rate that a Bank participant would have to pay. In this sense, then, the excess of R over i is the cost to a borrower for the privilege of possibly paying even less than i, made possible by the contingent-repayment nature of the Bank. For students who expect low incomes, $(R - i)$ is probably irrelevant; they will join as long as τ seems reasonable. But borrowers who expect high incomes will only join if the insurance is priced reasonably, that is, if they do not regard $(R - i)$ as excessive.[18] Given the assumption that those who expect high income will actually earn more, it follows that Y falls as $(R - i)$ is raised. Equation 4 reflects income of the average borrower, but also stands for the extent of participation in the Bank. This follows from the assumption that only those who expect high income vary their participation; those who expect low income always join.[19]

In summation, the system of equations implied by this Bank, using assumptions similar to those of Shell, are:

$$\tau = f(r, R, Y)$$
$$+ - -$$

(1a)

$$R = r + k$$

(2)

$$r = i - s$$

(3)

$$Y = g(R - i)$$
$$- +$$

(4)

---

[18] A word of caution here. We are using i to represent both the "cost of funds to the Bank" and "what the borrower would have to pay for a conventional (guaranteed) loan." To the extent that the Educational Opportunity Bank could attract capital at lower prices than an alternative guaranteed loan program (if one existed) there would be a divergence between these two borrowing rates. However, since the Bank's cost of funds could be expected to change with any general market rate, the major effect of our simplification is that $(R - i)$ should be read as an "index of the price of insurance" rather than as the absolute value of the price.

[19] Equation 4 could be rewritten to account explicitly for the effect of τ on the participation rate of students. Instead, the possibility of a high τ discouraging participation is discussed as a special case below.

The Bank manager contemplates setting terms for the Bank as follows: The capital market determines i, the interest cost of the Bank. From this rate, the manager subtracts the agreed-upon rate of subsidy, s. This difference determines the required rate of return of the Bank, r (equation 3). Given r, the manager adds the accustomed markup, k, to maintain the spread between R and r (equation 2). The number and expected income of Bank participants is now estimated from equation 4, using the opt-out rate, R, determined in the last step.

Having now determined r, R, and Y, the Bank can set τ by solving equation 1a. Unlike the situation described by Shell, however, it is possible that τ will be much higher than anticipated and/or that very few participants with expected high incomes will join the Bank. That is, if the opt-out rate, R, is set low enough to encourage participation by a sufficient number of income optimists in equation 4, k would have to be very low in equation 2 and, as Figure 6 demonstrates, τ will be high.[20] On the other hand if k is kept high in equation 2, the opt-out rate R may be so high that there will be intolerably few participants.

In this model of the Bank, one cannot guarantee simultaneously a low tax rate, a high level of participation, and an externally established rate of subsidy. One of these variables may have to give. The Bank has three choices:

1 It can guarantee high participation of income optimists by making $(R - i)$ very small and can guarantee relatively low tax rates by setting k very high. This choice implies that the rate of subsidization will be high.[21]

2 The Bank can select a low subsidy rate and a relatively high k, keeping the opt-out rate high, and insuring a low tax rate. In this case, the Bank will not attract high earners.

---

[20] I am assuming here that in the relevant range, an increase in k lowers τ in spite of the fact that it also lowers Y. In general, a change of k will raise or lower τ depending on the sign of the derivative of equation 1a with respect to k. That derivative is given by $d\tau/dk = \partial\tau/\partial R + \partial Y/\partial k \cdot \partial\tau/\partial Y$. The first term is negative and the second positive. I am assuming that the absolute value of the second term is less than that of the first.

[21] This says let $R - i = M$, in which M is a "small" constant while k is "large." From equation 2 we then have $r + k = M + i$ or $i - r = k - M$. But $i - r$ (from equation 3) equals s. So, $s = k - M$. If k is large and M is small, s is large.

3 It can guarantee sufficient participation of high earners and fix the subsidy rate at some externally determined small level. In this case, the tax rate may be much larger than is politically or economically acceptable.

None of these alternatives is particularly attractive.[22] The first case allows *the rate of subsidization of higher education to be determined ultimately by the willingness of students who expect high incomes to buy insurance* against the possibility of lower earnings. If these potential borrowers are relatively certain of high earnings or if they place little value on the income protection afforded by the Bank, the necessary rate of subsidy will be high. Of course, if those who expect high incomes are less certain of their prospects or if they value highly the kind of protection the Bank gives, they may be willing to join even at substantial spreads between the opt-out rate and the market interest rate. In that case, it may be possible to maintain a low subsidy. In any event, the *rate of subsidy to higher education should not be determined by the willingness of the population to buy income insurance,* but rather by the value that society places on the social benefits of higher education.

The present value of the subsidy in a 40-year loan is 10 to 15 percent of the loan principal for each percentage point of subsidized interest. At the "total student charges" levels, previously discussed, a 1.5 percentage point subsidy would have cost the federal government about $1.5 billion in 1967–68, rising to over $3 billion in 1977–78. If a comprehensive Bank attempts to finance "full costs," a 1.5 percentage point subsidy implies total federal subsidies twice as large. Shell never explicitly states a subsidy rate, but if we assume that $(R - i)$ is kept small, the implicit subsidy in his tables is on the order of 1.5–2.0 percentage points.

The second possible strategy for the Bank is to set the opt-out rate very high and limit federal subsidies. This strategy implies that the Bank will not attract sufficient numbers of people who expect high earnings. In a recent note, Shell (1970, pp. 214–220) examined the implications of a Bank with these characteristics.

[22] Quantitative trade-offs among tax rates, opt-out rates, and rates of return are examined for Canada by Cook and Stager (1969) with special reference to the Province of Ontario.

Shell demonstrates that even if the highest earners participate at only about half the rate of the lowest earners (when the price of insurance $[R - i]$ is kept at 2 percent),[23] the tax rate required for the Bank to break even is hardly affected. Put another way, if the Bank ignored the possibility of significant adverse selection of participants (thus setting τ too low), but such selection arose in practice, the losses of the Bank would be on the order of 3 percent of the Bank's annual interest cost.[24] The implication of this result is that there is very little internal redistribution within the Bank. Most borrowers end up fully requiting their own loans, and it is only in the very lowest tail of graduates' incomes that the "insurance" is ever cashed in.[25] It was perhaps for this reason that the National Student Loan Bank proposed in the Rivlin report was designed to make fixed-interest-rate loans, but allowed "for a limited form of . . . mutualization of risk. For any year in which a borrower's income falls below certain levels, a portion of the loan payment for that year would be cancelled. This feature could be designed to affect 5–10 percent of the scheduled repayments" of the Bank in any year (HEW, 1969c, pp. 32–33).[26]

The principal differences between this provision and the implicit subsidization in the Educational Opportunity Bank are:

a   The Rivlin report approach reduces the risk to the Bank itself by allowing the Bank to limit the dollar value of the cancellations, rather than make the cancellations depend on the selection of borrowers and their future incomes.

b   The subsidy paid to those who receive cancellations in the Rivlin report Bank is paid by the general (federal) taxpayer. In the Edu-

[23] In an unsubsidized Bank (that is, $i = r$).

[24] See Shell (1970, Table V, p. 219). In this table, Shell sets a target rate of return of 6 percent for the Bank. After accounting for adverse selection, the Bank's actual yield only falls to .058.

[25] This conclusion follows from the fact that the overall rate of return of the Bank must be the weighted average of the particular rates of return of the various income deciles. Shell's analysis asserts that even with a vast change in the weights attached to the particular rates of return, the overall rate is barely changed. Thus, the particular rates of return could not have differed very much in the first place.

[26] A similar provision, entailing deferral of payment in low-earning years is part of the Swedish study funds plan. See Swedish Institute (1968, p. 3). Deferral of repayment is also included in the revised recommendations of the Carnegie Commission on Higher Education. See Carnegie Commission (1970, p. 10).

cational Opportunity Bank, it is paid by successful borrowers, whose repayments to the Bank exceed the Bank's average rate of return.

It is not easy to decide who should pay the subsidies for the higher education of the lowest-earning college graduates. The reasons for the low earnings are some compound of tradition (low-earning college graduates participate disproportionately in traditionally low-paying occupations), discrimination, lack of motivation (they are more likely to be lazy), personal characteristics (they are more likely to be unpleasant or sickly), and luck. If these are the factors against which the Educational Opportunity Bank borrowers are protecting themselves, then it would seem just that they pay for the avoidance of the consequences of such factors. On the other hand, if this list represents general social risks or market imperfections not particularly associated with postsecondary education, the more appropriate subsidizing agent would be the federal taxpayer, and not those few borrowers who realize high earnings and are stuck with the bill under this version of the Educational Opportunity Bank.

The final choice described above is most difficult to evaluate. The Bank would insure Congress that subsidies will be limited and that the Bank will attract a cross section of the future income distribution by holding down R and limiting s. One critical question here is how high the tax rate might go, and how high tax rates might affect the political acceptability of the Bank.

To illustrate this case, suppose that the Bank's cost of raising funds is 6.4 percent (not at all unreasonable by 1969–70 standards). Congress limits the subsidy to 1 percentage point, meaning that the Bank must schedule its taxes so as to earn an average rate of return, r, of 5.4 percent. Suppose that an opt-out rate of 6.5 percent is adequate to attract enough high-income earners to justify the assumptions made by Shell in his original article (that participation will be independent of future income). Then, given Shell's assumptions about income growth, taxation of females, and so forth, the required tax rate per \$1,000 borrowed is 1.0 percent, that is, $\tau = 1.0$.[27] The average full-time equivalent student in 1967–68 would borrow about \$1,460 from the Bank if all other subsidies existent in 1967–68 were maintained and

---

[27] The description in this paragraph corresponds to Shell's Table IV.6 (1968, p. 22). The repayment period is 40 years.

only student charges were financed at the Bank. Over a four-year college career, total borrowings would amount to about $6,000, and the education tax surcharge would be 6.0 percent of income. Interestingly enough, this percent of income is just at the stringent repayment ceiling identified in Chapter 2 of this report. However, if the average student were to have borrowed "full costs," as defined in Appendix A, a four-year college career, commencing in 1967–68, would have implied about an 11 percent surcharge on income over 40 years. For a family with a mother with a bachelor's degree and a father with a doctoral degree (2 years above undergraduate), it would rise to 29 percent.[28]

The first question to raise about tax rates of such apparently high magnitude is whether substantial numbers of students would actually join such a Bank, as these tax rates go well beyond the range of any existing program. It is possible that this variant of the Bank could never get off the ground.

The second question to raise is how to evaluate such a Bank, if it were the source of a massive shift in the financing of higher education. The estimates of repayment ceilings in Chapter 2 presuppose a certain level of state and local taxes to support higher education. But state and local taxation would clearly be reduced if a full-cost Bank replaced the present heavy reliance on state-supported institutions. Some groups would gain and others lose from such a shift in higher education finance, with resulting social implications.

1   A full-cost Educational Opportunity Bank would shift costs from state and local taxpayers to federal taxpayers and to Bank borrowers.

2   Since college students are now—and will likely in the future continue to be—from families that are wealthier than the tax-paying population in general, financial support is shifted to a group with greater ability to pay.

---

[28] See Table 1 for the cost data in this paragraph. Similar calculations for the "total student charges" model would cut these family tax rates approximately in half. The estimates assume that wives earn no income. In the Bank described by Shell women pay bank tax on their own income if that income exceeds the average for women. If a wife's income is below that level, she pays part of the bank tax and her husband pays part out of his income. If the wife is without income, the husband assumes the wife's tax *rate* and applies it to his (family) income (see Shell et al., 1968, pp. 16ff).

3 Since the state-local tax system is regressive, especially at lower incomes (Hansen & Weisbrod, 1969, p. 75), the reduced reliance on state-local taxpayers would be twice-blessed: Not only is this group poorer than Bank borrowers, but the poorer members of the group are presently more heavily taxed. The lesser reliance on state institutions may be thrice-blessed, if, as Hansen & Weisbrod contend, the subsidies granted by state institutions are absolutely larger for wealthier college students than for poorer ones (Hansen & Weisbrod, 1969, p. 76) (although wealthier borrowers may borrow from the Bank and thus receive larger absolute subsidies from the federal government).

4 The federal taxpayer picks up part of the burden yielded by state and local taxpayers. Since the federal tax system is progressive, an additional argument can be made for the Bank's conformity with the ability-to-pay doctrine. (This would hold for any shift in financing from state and local revenues to federal.)

5 Most of the reduction in reliance on state and local taxation would be compensated for by an increase in taxes of Bank borrowers. It has already been indicated that these borrowers in general are richer than state and local taxpayers.[29]

The only remaining question is what is the incidence of taxation *among borrowers* at the Bank? Assuming, for simplicity, that all borrowers borrow the same sum, *tax repayments to the Bank will be proportional to income up to a certain level and then become sharply regressive.* The reason for this regressivity at higher incomes is that the opt-out rate puts a ceiling on tax payments. Thus, any taxpayer whose income is high enough to warrant opting-out will do so, *and so will everyone whose income is higher than this level.* Millionaires pay no more in bank taxes than do the college graduates for whom opting-out is marginally profitable. The bank-tax system is, at least in the highest income ranges, more regressive than state-local or federal tax systems.

Dropping the assumption that everyone borrows the same amount at the Bank upsets the neatness of the argument. But the

[29] They are also of a later generation. The question of intergenerational burdens is being sloughed over here, although the transition to a full-cost Bank would certainly pose some equity problems. Any college graduate living at the time the Bank is established receives a windfall. He neither paid full cost, nor will he pay state and local taxes to subsidize future college students. The argument in the text treats families as timeless.

principle is maintained. Within each group of borrowers whose average loan is the same, the most successful members will pay the same tax as the marginal opter-outer in that group.

In summary, then, a full-cost Educational Opportunity Bank that attempts to attract a substantial part of the college-going population to its doors, and which provides a modest federal subsidy,[30] shifts costs from a poorer (general taxpayer) group to a richer (college-goer) one. However, the greatest gainers within the college-going group are those with the very highest incomes whose taxes are limited by the privileges of opting-out of the Bank. On the other hand, the lowest-earning college graduates stand to gain from the Bank because they need never repay the full costs of their borrowing. The inescapable conclusion, therefore, is that the biggest losers in the substitution of bank for state financing are the middle-income college-goers. Their group (college-goers) loses out from the substitution, but the very high earners and the very low earners in the group gain.

Evaluation of a Bank with the characteristics just described depends on the weights one attaches to the welfare of the various groups described. It also depends on precise definitions of some of the weasel words I have used here. Just how large is the group of college-goers for whom opting-out provides a cheap form of taxation? What is their income? How much must borrowers earn to allow them to repay less than the full cost of a college education? These important questions have not yet been answered.

CANCELLATIONS OF TEACHER LOANS UNDER NDSL The regulations governing the National Defense Student Loan program summarize the purpose of the teacher-cancellation provisions as being "designed to attract an additional number of superior students to the teaching profession" (HEW, 1967, Appendix 2, p. 1). The cancellations were reviewed in a study conducted by the College Entrance Examination Board, which was "unable to find any clear-cut evidence that the teacher cancellation provision has materially contributed to an increase in either the number or quality of teachers" and concluded that "the teacher cancellation provision . . . be phased out by eliminating the availability of this feature to new borrowers" (*Notes*

[30] The federal subsidy in this case would be between \$1 and 2 billion at the 1967–68 levels of full cost (\$13.8 billion, from Table 1), assuming a subsidy of 1 percent of interest or 10 to 15 percent of loan principal.

and Working Papers, 1968, pp. 46, 50).[31] On the key point of attracting students (any student—not necessarily "superior") to the teaching profession, the study group found that the rate of increase in classroom teachers had closely paralleled the rate of increase in high school graduates (four years earlier) both before and after the inception of the NDSL program. Thus, it is argued, lack of evidence that the program satisfies its direct goal is sufficient reason for dropping the cancellation provision.

There are several even stronger arguments for eliminating teacher cancellations.

First, evidence is accumulating that there is no need to offer special incentives to young people to enter the teaching profession. Both at the elementary and secondary level, and in colleges, projections of faculty supply do not fall short of demand.[32]

Although shortages may occur in specific subject fields, or in certain geographic areas, these are inefficiently treated with a blunt instrument like teacher cancellations. Moreover, other instruments exist and are being used—namely, the various provisions under Title V (Education Professions Development) of the Higher Education Act of 1965.[33] These programs allow the U.S. Office of Education, in principle, to attack shortages "now," rather than hope that a student financial-aid officer can predict a shortage area four years later and then find a student who plans to enter that field.

Even if cancellation of loans were the only available instrument for increasing the supply of teachers, the annual value of the cancellation to individuals is so small that it is virtually ineffectual. In fiscal 1968, the average annual cancellation for first-time teachers was $122.14, or less than 2 percent of average teacher salaries.[34] Teachers in schools with high concentrations

---

[31] This section borrows freely from the College Board Study (*Notes and Working Papers,* 1968).

[32] See HEW (1968, p. 2) and literature cited there. A shortage of elementary and secondary school teachers in the 1970s occurs only under extreme assumptions. For the college level, see Cartter (1966, pp. 22–38).

[33] In fiscal year 1969, these programs, including Teacher Corps, fellowships, and training programs, were budgeted at over $100 million. See *The Budget of the United States Government, Fiscal Year 1971* (Appendix, p. 428).

[34] U.S. Office of Education "Annual Report of Repayments on National Defense Students Loans," (n.d.). Cancellations were even smaller for experienced teachers.

of children from low-income families or teachers of the handi-capped are eligible for an additional annual cancellation of 5 percent (above the basic cancellation of 10 percent). It is unlikely that an additional $60 a year ($1.50 per school week) will lure many into a priority teaching area.[35]

Even if these small monetary incentives were considered effective and superior to alternatives, the question must be considered whether they are worth, in addition to the $20 million annual cost of cancellations (canceled repayments in fiscal 1968), the secondary abuses unleashed by teacher cancellations, which are discussed below.

1   College financial aid officers apparently attempt to maximize the "grant-value" of National Defense Student Loans (that is, they lend to those who are most likely to use cancellations in the future). This is indicated by the fact that 45 percent of NDSL borrowers are female,[36] considerably in excess of either the female proportion of college students or the ratio of female borrowers under GLP (36 percent). With perfect forecasting of likely future teachers, college-aid officers could convert NDSL into a grant program under the guise of a loan program. Recent data indicate that this may be happening. In fiscal 1967, there were about 163,000 loans in the grace period (that is, first year after studies completed). In fiscal 1968, first-time teacher cancellations totaled 60,000. Since many "grace period" borrowers must have been dropouts or in military service, first-time teachers probably account for over half of all recent NDSL graduates, implying a shrinking rate of growth of NDSL repayments in the future.

2   The most common repayment schedule "selected" by NDSL borrowers involves periodic repayment of a *constant amount of principal* plus interest on the outstanding balance. In other words, borrowers have been "selecting" to repay *declining* absolute sums over the course of their repayment period. It is inconceivable that borrowers, no matter how ill-informed, would really prefer to make their heaviest repayments in early years. (However, the

---

[35] There is an additional advantage to the teacher eligible for 15 percent can-cellation—he may eventually cancel his entire loan, while the 10 percent annual canceler is limited to canceling only half of his loan. See *Notes and Working Papers* (1968, p. 45).

[36] Statement of Representative Edith Green (*Congressional Record,* daily edi-tion, October 16, 1969, p. H. 9649).

accumulated debt of the average borrower has been quite small, so the initial and final payments are not enormously different). *The reason for this unusual selection of repayment terms is that it is the simplest one for financial aid officers to manage when there are teacher cancellations.*[37] Indeed, the *Manual of Policies and Procedures for the NDSL* program strongly hints that plans providing for "equal payments of *principal* only, plus payment of the exact amount of interest which has accrued on the unpaid balance . . . are particularly suitable for borrowers who will be eligible for teacher cancellation" (HEW, 1967, p. 43).

3   The value of the time spent in establishing and administering the detailed rules of teacher cancellation is staggering. Those provisions have been responsible for as much as 80 percent of the correspondence and inquiries in the loans section at the U.S. Office of Education (*Notes and Working Papers,* 1968, pp. 49–50). Memoranda from the NDSL office to financial aid officers are dominated by clarifications of the teacher-cancellation provisions.[38] For the most part the administrative effort and paper work involved in these activities, while necessary under present law, are unproductive in any meaningful sense of the word.

Teacher cancellations are depriving today's college borrowers of over $20 million in loan funds. The total is growing rapidly. The program serves no legitimate purpose. It involves wasteful use of administrative time and encourages abuses in the student financial aid system. There is no bigger roadblock to converting the NDSL program into a program serving the goal of enhanced higher education opportunity for low-income students.

---

[37] On a 10-year loan, with equal periodic repayment of principal, exactly 10 percent of the total principal falls due in the first year. This sum, plus interest, represents the allowable cancellations for teachers. On the other hand, equal total (principal plus interest) periodic payments will result in less than 10 percent of principal falling due in the first year, necessitating a recalculation of the entire repayment schedule if the borrower obtains a teacher cancellation.

[38] Example: Athletic coaches in colleges are eligible for cancellations; medical staff is not.

7. Conference Summary

Thirty-five economists, bankers, educators, and government officials met at The Brookings Institution in April 1970 to discuss problems of existing college student loan programs and proposals for change. The conference participants' experiences ranged from administering loan programs on a campus or in financial institutions to a purely academic interest in the financing of higher education.

The conference was organized around three themes: (a) the role of the government in financing higher education, (b) optimum characteristics of student loans, and (c) organization of capital markets and administrative procedures for student loans.

THE ROLE OF GOVERNMENT IN FINANCING HIGHER EDUCATION

If there is a litmus test to predict whether a person is an enthusiast or an opponent of expansion of loans for college students, that test would be his conception of the role of government in higher education finance.[1] Two polar views represented at the conference were:

- Government has a very limited role to play in financing higher education. A relatively larger burden must therefore be assumed by students and their families. Loans are an acceptable vehicle for spreading that burden over time.

- It is a major responsibility of government to subsidize higher education. Students will thus need relatively little current financing. Student loans should therefore remain unattractive to borrowers lest they tempt government decision makers to withdraw the necessary subsidies.

[1] One of the ground rules in the conference discussion was that "higher education finance" did not include financing research activities. This omission will be maintained here. A list of conference participants appears in Appendix E.

There is not much prospect of compromise between these two positions, and, although each is an exaggeration of most participants' beliefs, the heat of debate induced some exaggerated views. As a result, all participants in the conference rarely were on one side of any given issue. It is, however, worthwhile to review the reasons why conference participants adopted such diverse views. The reasons largely reflected the relative value participants attached to the government goals of equal opportunity, greater access to credit, and compensating for social benefits of higher education discussed in the introduction to this report.

Equal Opportunity Many participants saw the principal role of government in higher education to be the achievement of equal opportunity. For most participants, the operational counterpart of this goal was to insure that students from lower-income families could afford some form of higher education, but some participants argued that the government's responsibility extended further: to provide lower-income and higher-income students with the same range of choice of type of institution.

Among those who emphasized enrollment equalization, there was a strong view that this governmental objective could only be served through grants to students. There was extreme pessimism that loan programs could be tailored to "fit the needs" of youngsters from low-income families. The government would have to provide such students with scholarships; loans, at most, could provide leeway for greater choice among institutions.

On the other hand, one participant argued that if government is concerned with greater enrollments of students from very low-income (that is, poverty) families, large, generous loan programs may be a necessity. He observed that such students would require aid not only for explicit expenses of college-going but for a substantial portion of their forgone earnings as well. Inasmuch as no one has proposed—or is likely to propose—grant programs sufficient to compensate for forgone earnings as well as expenses, it follows that student loans of considerable magnitude will be necessary.

The need to provide low-income students with funds sufficient to offset a substantial portion of forgone earnings in order to induce them to attend postsecondary institutions stems from two factors. First is their alleged extreme unwillingness to give up present enjoyments even for large future gains. (The time expended in college studies would, however, preempt most concurrent satisfactions even if forgone earnings were available.) Second, it has been argued that low-income youth are expected to help support their parental families. If that is the case, government grants "to students" are indirect welfare payments to their families, and government loans "to students" are "reverse inheritances," in which the child "leaves" some money to his parents out of the capital he is accumulating.

Subsidizing for Social Benefits

One group of participants clearly placed great emphasis on the government's role as protector of the social benefits of higher education. According to this view, students cannot and should not be made to pay for those aspects of their education which result in benefits that are widely diffused throughout society. Government should "pay the costs" associated with the greater political participation by the citizenry, the cultural leadership, and kindred effects of higher education. Since these benefits are jointly produced with other more private benefits of higher schooling, it is difficult to establish how large the social-benefit costs are or which students cause such costs to be incurred.

Under these circumstances, most participants who emphasized the importance of government's role in compensating for social benefits favor low tuition, which spreads government subsidies pretty evenly among students in all income groups. From this perspective, loans for students take on a very limited, supplementary role.

One participant illustrated a federal government policy consistent with this point of view as follows: The federal government has an obligation to offer subsidized support to *all* students. It is all right to have programs that target aid toward low-income students, but an obligation also exists to help the middle-class student. (Indeed, it was contended that grant programs for the poor make them better off than the middle class, or at least, that it is inequitable to aid the poor student without giving something to the middle class.) Loan programs, with subsidized interest rates for the middle class, were viewed from this perspective as a pragmatic response to a legitimate federal objective. Participants holding this view seemed to give high priority to expanding significantly the availability of subsidized loan funds for all students (especially through the National Defense Student Loan program).

Even with dramatic expansion in availability of subsidized loans, it is not likely that all students would borrow. If the intent of the loan subsidy is to have the federal government share in the costs of providing social benefits, then a selective loan program raises the issue of horizontal equity. Why should the government subsidize more heavily those who borrow more and not at all those who fail to borrow? It was not clear from the conference discussion whether advocates accepted this apparent incongruity as the price of a practical compromise or whether it was an intended discrimination among students.

Another view consistent with the emphasis on federal subsidization for all students amounted to an extension of the principles governing secondary education in the United States. Thus, the first two years of college should be fully subsidized by the government, and universal attendance should be encouraged, although compulsion to attend need not be introduced. Beyond this basic level of postsecondary education (one participant argued that the basic level should be four years), higher education should be viewed as a selective and specialized collection of enterprises where the government should draw distinctions and tailor loan programs to fit each case. For example, some forms of schooling beyond the basic level are clearly and primarily vocational training, designed to facilitate entry into a profession. In these cases, the government's role should be limited to providing access to credit without subsidy of interest (see next section). On the other hand, some forms of education beyond the basic level really amount to support of research, and the fact that degrees are granted is incidental to this basic purpose. In such cases, the criteria for public support should be based on an evaluation of government's role in research support, and questions of equal opportunity, access to credit, and so on would be beside the point.

Access to Credit

The point of view just described conveniently spills over into the third broad grouping of participants' philosophies.

Some participants in the conference maintained that the benefits of college training accrue predominantly, if not exclusively, to the student in the form of increased future income. All of postsecondary education, therefore, can be considered as investment in capital assets. This group of participants considered the sole justification for government loan programs to be to perfect a laissez-faire capital market. Thus, the only subsidies should be government insuring of student loans (to compensate for the market imperfection caused by the impossibility of repossessing human capital). In addition, loan programs should provide for some form of risk-sharing (to compensate for the failure of private insurers to enter this market). Some participants argued that risk-sharing arrangements (such as scaling repayment requirements to future income) encouraged greater enrollment by students whose parental incomes were low, and that would be an extra "plus" for the loan program. But such results were not the raison d'être of contingent repayments.

Few participants suggested that no compromise was possible on the all-benefits-are-private point of view. Indeed, it was argued that the practical best loan program is the one which comes closest to a perfected capital market, even it if requires some deviations from the economic optimum. So, for example, if it is necessary to continue some subsidies to interest rates as the price for an expanding, longer term, income-contingent loan program, the price should be paid. Part of the conference proceedings was devoted to discussing departures from the optimum necessary to attract a viable political coalition, but little agreement was reached on either the identity of the political actors or on their response coefficients to alternative student aid packages.

The conference discussion of the role of government in student loans hardly resulted in any consensus, but consensus is probably not possible, since the issues involved touch upon fundamental values about government, the distribution of opportunity, and the autonomy of educational institutions, among others. Moreover, an individual's attitude about the federal government's role depends in part upon the expected behavior of state and local governments and the development of secondary and postgraduate education.

Against the background of diversity in assessing government's role, the conference turned to the ideal properties of a federal student loan program.

OPTIMUM CHARACTER-ISTICS OF STU-DENT LOANS

Three characteristics of student loans occupied most of the attention of the conferees: subsidies in loans, length of repayment term, and income-contingent repayments.

Subsidies in Loans

As indicated above, most conference participants agreed that a substantial grant program, not tied to loans, would be necessary to induce students from poor and near-poor families, particularly among racial minorities, to continue their education beyond high school. Conference participants "in the field" were particularly vehement about low-income students' aversion to loans.

Some examples of the debate:

University official "HEW has been encouraging the acceleration of admission of disadvantaged students to our institutions. We have worked very hard for over a decade . . . in this area and we have had very good results. . . . Having talked with a large number of these people — talking to them about loans for education is just impossible. They really are not in conversation with us at all. . . . I am quite clear in my mind that if we are going to meet this issue, grant programs will be the only way it will work out and with some of these young people as they move to years three and four would consider loan programs."

Government official "All over the country colleges that are bringing in disadvantaged students . . . have got to teach them what it is to borrow. . . . Upward Bound and programs of this kind begin this indoctrination. . . . This would have to occur to get the disadvantaged students to accept — even a subsidized loan — but that seems to be a job that a lot of people are taking on with some success. . . ."

University official "He is not going to go for the loan. We have to be crystal clear that it is a grant program."

Government official "Then the basic question is whether there is a role for subsidized loans in between grants and unsubsidized loans."

University official "I say grants should have the priority."

Economist "Even with medical school students, there is a tremendous resistance on the part of a lot of people and particularly poor people with respect to being saddled with loans. . . . Students simply regarded loans . . . as a device to impose involuntary servitude on them. They accused [loan proponents] of discriminating against the poor and the blacks. . . ."

University official "You might be able to make that same student a loan in his third year of medical school . . . where he can see some of the advantages of his education. . . . The poor are not going to be encouraged by any talk of loans at all. If we want to move up to the middle-income group then of course they are going to be borrowing, but the best way to scare them from borrowing is talking about indenturing them for forty years."

Economist "I would like to distinguish between two different elements in this, one of which I can understand and maybe even agree with in some sense. The other I simply don't understand.

"The first element is a purely political judgment. If I were a poor black student who had been admitted to medical school I might feel 'There is justification for white society to be paying me to go to medical school. It is a scandal that it should have the continued brass to make me . . . take out a loan for this. . . .' That is a political judgment about the rights and wrongs of the situation.

"If the reason for resistance, however, is that the newly admitted student doesn't have any clear notion of how much his income is going to increase . . . that if he doesn't go through medical school . . . his income will stay at a low level and if he goes to medical school, even if he is black, he will move into the upper decile of the income distribution . . . then that should be susceptible of rational explanation."

One interesting insight into the role of attitudes toward loans was the experience of the government study assistance program in Sweden. Relying on assumptions about attitudes similar to those expressed above, that country has had a substantial grant program for low-income students, in addition to loans. As the program has developed, however, grants to students whose *parents* are poor have been reduced, as it becomes more generally recognized that these students will be high earners (Directorate for Scientific Affairs, 1967, pp. 203–206, 211–214, 327–328). As a result, Sweden is moving toward a more comprehensive loan program with subsidies reserved only for those students whose *own* (future) incomes are low. Whether such contingent subsidies will be effective in inducing enrollments among the lower-income group in Sweden, and whether the experience is applicable to the United States was not readily apparent to the conference participants.

Given a grant program of sufficient capacity, the arguments for and against subsidized interest rates in federal loan programs were presented as follows:

For The National Defense Student Loan program and the Guaranteed Loan Program have passed the test of congressional and public political survival. If we accept that subsidies to higher education are a legitimate — or as legitimate as any other — government activity, then these programs are suitable vehicles because they are on the books. Moreover, neither program proved to be administratively simple at inception, but improvements have been made. New programs would have to be tried for a while at unknown costs. Finally, building a political coalition is not a simple matter of efficiency and matching goals and benefits and costs; a viable coalition is a fragile, historically and even accidentally bound phenomenon. Subsidies in existing federal loan programs have satisfied the coalition test.

Against   The fact remains that no one has ever demonstrated what qualities are possessed by student borrowers and their colleges that warrant subsidies while nonborrowers and their institutions get none. Even if virtually all students borrowed, no one has demonstrated why the size of the subsidy should vary with the size of the loan. History of past political battles and of valiant fights does not obviate the inequities of misallocating hundreds of millions of dollars. Building a viable coalition is relevant, but if we cannot distinguish between viable coalitions for sensible programs and for wasteful ones, a sad day is upon us.

Length of Re-
payment Term
The background paper for the conference approached the subject of the length of the repayment period from the point of view of "equity" or "oppressiveness of burden on the borrower." This approach was criticized from two sides. Economists at the conference tended to approach student loans from investment theory, while practitioners emphasized implications of lengthened repayment terms for the supply of capital.

The investment theory approach can be summarized as follows. Consider the student at age eighteen to be contemplating a college education. Ignoring explicit charges for higher education, he would have to determine whether the income he forgoes during his college years would be sufficiently offset by the higher income he would earn after college. By analogy with a firm, the student would plot a chart into his future showing his cumulative income over time with and without a college education. Since future income is less highly valued than present income, the student would discount the future earnings in constructing his cumulative-earnings profiles.

What would the charts look like? Without college, cumulative earnings would start immediately, but rise relatively slowly. With college, the student would have four years of low earnings, after which cumulative earnings would mount rapidly. If college training is worthwhile to the student, then the two charts will cross in the future as the college-trained student's cumulative earnings exceed those of the high school graduate. One conference participant concluded from this analysis that:

. . . the net payoff of college attendance and completion is concentrated in the latter part of the working life of the student. . . . This is true even for undiscounted cumulative income, and it becomes still more true if the student, as he rationally should, engages in some discounting of the two alternative income streams. . . .[A]ll loan financing for which the re-payment is concentrated in the early years of working life—say, the first ten years after graduation—has some deterrent effect upon college atten-dance. . . . [If] loan financing is heavily relied on, the deterrent effect of loans with a short payment period cannot fail to be substantial. The shorter the repayment period . . . the greater is the rational discouragement to the student. . . . The first problem he faces is the risk of a net loss in the event he fails to complete college work but still has debt hanging over him to be paid off out of a cumulative income stream that is lower than it would have been had he completed college work. Furthermore, the student who does not have an optimistic forecast for future [incremental] income or who has a high subjective discount rate is relatively more discouraged by an op-portunity only to finance his education with loans having a short repayment period. . . .

The conference participants who accepted the investment charac-ter of student loans went on to argue that the appropriate terms for such loans should "coincide with the working life-time," or some 40 years for most users of higher education.

The principal objection to lengthening the repayment term of loans beyond where they presently stand is the cost of servicing loans. Several conference participants argued that increased lend-ing to students by financial institutions is deterred largely by the high costs of servicing loans and by the slow turnover of principal on student loans. They pointed out that 40-year terms would worsen both of these features significantly and would make banks even less eager for this type of lending activity. If the additional service and liquidity costs of repayment lengthening were added to the student's bill, and if interest subsidies were eliminated as had been suggested by some, the repayment rates might well move into a range that was politically and/or socially unacceptable. Even if higher education financed through very long-term loans could be proved to be "profitable" to both borrowers and lenders, the changes in home-ownership patterns, for example, that might be induced by "repaying two mortgages" might be unacceptable. Proponents of short repayment terms warned participants who wanted greater reliance on loans to finance students not to eliminate exactly those features of present loan programs that made the market appealing to lenders and to the Congress.

Many of the differences on the length of the repayment period seemed to hinge on the conference participants' perception of the future importance of loans. If loans were to continue as a fairly minor adjunct to other financing methods, the repayment term becomes a less critical issue. Most students will not be discouraged from continuing their education by a short repayment requirement. On the other hand, if a longer repayment option were offered to the few students who want to borrow heavily, capital markets could hardly be expected to turn away from all student loans because of the option.

If loans become the major means of financing student charges, than present repayment terms cannot be reasonably defended. If changes in the lending institutions are required to induce them to lend at longer term, then such changes will have to be made. If higher rates to borrowers are required, they will have to be paid. If larger repayment requirements cause adjustments in home-ownership patterns, then financial practices in the mortgage market will have to be changed.

It is neither an argument for nor against longer repayment terms to indicate that such changes would affect financial markets and other activities. The point is that large changes in the means of financing any important economic activity must change other activities as long as markets are interrelated. The decision must first be made whether loans are to become a more important means of financing higher education. If they are, changes in loan repayment terms will be required, and such changes may necessitate accommodations in other financial markets and institutions.

One compromise on loan repayment terms was proposed at the conference, but inadequately discussed. The suggestion was made that current (or slightly longer) repayment terms be made the "standard." Students whose accumulated debt rose above certain pre-established levels could exercise the option of extending repayment terms, perhaps with an additional charge. This proposal has the virtue of accommodating to the needs of high-debt students without necessarily throwing the whole student loan market into higher cost practices.

Income-contingent Repayments

Considering that the hottest debate in higher education finance circles in recent years centered on the Educational Opportunity Bank proposed by the Zacharias panel (see Chapters 1 and 6), discussion of income-contingent repayment plans at the Carnegie-Brookings conference was surprisingly mild. The conferees were asked to isolate in their minds whether student loan repayments (or cancellation of repayments) should be based on income—given an arrangement with respect to interest charges, length of repayment period, and eligibility for loans. Thus segregated, the income-contingent repayment plans were discussed primarily under the rubric of risk-reduction.

There are several kinds of risks against which some form of income-related repayment scheme could protect borrowers. One conference participant suggested a hierarchy of risks and loan repayment plans as follows (italics added):

At the lowest level one can have a fixed plan in which each borrower repays what he himself has borrowed at a fixed rate of interest, the only concession being that those who *have low incomes* in one or more years would be able to defer the repayment and extend [the loan term] and the people who fail to repay would be people who over their entire lifetime fail to have an income to make [full] repayment at a feasible burden. . . .

Second would be . . . a fixed repayment schedule but in *years of low-income* the repayment due would be *entirely forgiven* instead of deferred. This is the kind of repayment that [would ensue] if repayment were in terms of a percentage of income. . . .

[A] more extreme suggestion is the full equity principle in which the student is selling shares in the added earning power that he is getting through his education. . . . At each stage of the game you are telling the person who is borrowing "this is a no cure-no pay proposition. If you continue your education and it doesn't result in your having higher income, you don't pay. If it is successful, the people who have backed you have an equity interest in your earnings. . . .

One could develop a large number of [plans] and a person could have a choice of various kinds of contracts that he could enter into ranging from the almost flat loan with only the examination for low income all the way up to the [full equity] extreme.

The participants never really grappled with either the benefits or the costs of such approaches. Some participants expressed no real objection to providing at least limited forms of insurance, but questioned whether the costs and complications of introducing income-related repayment schemes were worth the alleged benefits. It is interesting to note that in a poll of participants, the economists at the conference were preponderantly in favor of some form of income-related repayments, while bankers and college officials were, on the whole, opposed. It is probably a fair guess that the degree of commitment to income-contingent repayments is related to how strongly one feels "investment strategy" is (and should be) the decision criterion for college attendance.

The question of "what to do about women" arose in the context of the income-related repayments discussion. Some participants expressed the view that any program for financing higher education through loans would ipso facto discriminate against women, who could not afford repayments if they chose to remain in the home. A more moderate view was that loan deferrals or cancellations could be used to compensate families during child-bearing or child-rearing years. At the opposite pole, the view was expressed that no distinction should be made between the sexes and that joint family income was the relevant measure of ability to pay, no matter how many earners contributed to that income. There was no evident consensus on this question.

CAPITAL MARKETS AND ADMINISTRATIVE PROCEDURES The conference participants devoted relatively little time to the possibility of meeting the capital needs of student loans through direct appropriations, although several participants indicated that in their view "on the budget" solutions were conceptually similar to "off the budget" plans. One conferee characterized the "off the budget" philosophy as *après moi, le deluge,* and warned that Washington was filled with conferences trying to devise similar evasive financing schemes for other domestic activities. In any event, the conference agenda was devoted to raising capital through private markets.

There was general agreement that the present institutional framework of the Guaranteed Loan Program would not be adequate to student loan requirements in the long run. Two aspects of the existing program were emphasized: the lack of a flexible interest rate and strong reliance on commercial banks under the present program.[2] The following dialogue summarizes the problems succinctly:

Banker A "*The New York Times* this morning had advertisements for installment loans, car loans—and car loans are commanding a 10 to 12 percent rate—so apparently banks in New York are looking for . . . loans at a rate between 10 and 12 percent. . . . If there is an artificial rate [for student loans]—and indeed there is—[money] is going to go where the free market permits us to get the highest rate."

[2] The variable special allowance of 0 to 3 percent of the Emergency Insured Student Loan Act of 1969 (P.L. 91–95, enacted in October 1969) had not been tested at the time of the Brookings conference. The peak loan season is August and September.

Banker B "Even if you had a free market rate, since such a high proportion of [student] loans are made by commercial banks then you will have periods in which monetary policy is tight, banks will be squeezed, and a free rate won't solve the situation. . . . There is a remarkable parallelism between student loans and the whole mortgage market . . . and this leads into the whole idea of a secondary market. . . ."

Indeed, the pros and cons of a secondary market became the central issue in the discussion. A broad definition of secondary markets was adopted: A secondary market means that an independent institution would be organized to raise capital in exchange for its own securities and for a fee would provide funds to originating lenders out of the proceeds. In principle, the annual net lending of a secondary institution can be small or large relative to the total student loan market; it can make partial advances against student loans or purchase such loans outright. The conference discussion did not probe these alternatives deeply, and most of the discussion seemed to be based on the stronger alternatives: larger volume, outright purchase.

Some of the conference participants expressed doubt that a secondary market would significantly enhance the flow of capital into student loans. They stressed the interrelation of capital markets, arguing that if the secondary-market institution raised $X through issue of its own securities, there would be $X less flowing to other institutions, thereby impairing these institutions' ability to lend to students. The argument continues that there is really only a single (real) pool of credit, limited at any (full-employment) time by the voluntary savings of individuals and governments, and that a secondary market will allow easier stealing from Peter to pay Paul. Implicit in this view is that Peter's needs for housing, schools, and factories should not be slighted for Paul's sheepskin.

The counter view is more optimistic. First, it is acknowledged that if a secondary market works—that is, enhances the flow of funds into student loans—it will divert funds from other sectors. Such diversion can be accomplished, in pure form, either by taxation and direct government appropriation of the revenues or by free market forces bidding capital away from other sectors. The Guaranteed Loan Program already represents an impure form of diversion of resources by using the power of the state to change the terms (government guarantee reduces risk) on a particular class of loans. The establishment of a secondary market would merely extend this special treatment one step further by making student loans *more liquid.* In addition, the secondary market would allow investors who desire, for whatever reason, to invest in student loans to do so, without themselves servicing the loans.

The effectiveness of secondary-market intervention, it is argued, will then depend on whether lack of liquidity has been a serious barrier to the supply of capital and whether there are investors (such as those who buy Federal National Mortgage Association securities) who want to participate in government-guaranteed lending without themselves becoming lenders.

Against these positive influences is the possibility that savings flows will be diverted from institutions that would have made student loans with the diverted funds. Here it is important to distinguish student loans from home mortgages. There are institutions that specialize in residential loans, and if funds are diverted from these institutions to the capital issue of a secondary-market institution, much of the net inflow of funds into mortgages may be curtailed. In the case of student loans, however, while commercial banks predominate in student lending, student loans certainly do not predominate in bank portfolios (see Chapter 4). Thus, there is a strong chance that the establishment of a secondary-market institution for student loans will significantly increase the flow of capital into this sector.

After these preliminary discussions of the feasibility and desirability of establishing a secondary-market institution, the conference turned to two aspects of the supply side of the market: the relation between market interest rates and student loan rates, and the administration of loan programs.

Market Interest Rates and Student Loan Rates

A secondary-market institution would raise capital by issuing its own securities. These securities might be guaranteed by the federal government, or their attractiveness might be left to the fact that the assets of the institution are guaranteed student loans. The institution would borrow in both short-term and long-term markets at whatever interest rate is required to raise funds.

How would the rate of interest students pay be related to the market rate paid by the secondary-market institution? The conference discussion didn't get into details, but most conferees agreed that the interest rate charged to the student should move with the market. Those who favored subsidized interest for students implicitly argued that the subsidy differential should be maintained over time. Thus, one of the flaws in the government-backed home mortgage market—the retention of fixed minimum rates on Federal Housing Administration (FHA) mortgages—would be eliminated.

One exception to allowing student charges to vary was the preference on the part of some conference participants for stabilized rates. This was expressed as follows:

> . . . there would be a pretty powerful argument against having students who come out one year contracting their loans at a 9 percent rate and students who come out two years later contracting their loans at a 6 percent rate . . . you want something that smoothes it out. . . .

No explicit mechanism was discussed for smoothing charges, but it was clear that a government-supported fund could purchase student loan paper in times of unusually high market rates and sell the paper when rates drop below their secular trend, thus narrowing the range of potential rates charged to students.[3]

THE ADMINIS-TRATION OF LOAN PROGRAMS There was widespread support in the conference discussion of the principle that college and university financial-aid offices were the appropriate agencies to originate loans. The key points in favor of college origination were the accessibility of pertinent data—enrollment, expense, and (if necessary) family income records—to the financial-aid office and the greater likelihood that disadvantaged students would get a fair shake at the college if rationing of loans were necessary. These points were undisputed, but opposition arose to *adding* a new program of student loans administered by colleges, and financed through a secondary-market institution, to the already complicated existing student aid programs. Several participants with experience in loan administration argued for filling up existing cups with money rather than providing a new cup, no matter how shiny or big it would be. Advocates of a new program suggested the consolidation of at least some existing programs into a new loan plan—but the attractiveness of this proposal seemed to increase with the discussants' distance from government regulations and guidelines.

[3] The variation in rates paid by students who borrow in each of four years of college is the difference in four-year moving averages of interest rates. Using corporate (Aaa) bond yields to approximate market rates discloses that, in the 1960s, four-time borrowers graduating in succeeding years would never have paid more than 0.65 of 1 percent difference in rates. Even two-time borrowers' rates would not have differed by more than 0.76 of 1 percent.

On the question of servicing loans, the conferees again split along similar lines to the debate over origination. One group preferred central collections—through the Internal Revenue Service (IRS)—largely because the need to keep track of a very mobile population is the major element of cost in collecting repayments. Since mobility is a desirable attribute of highly educated people, this circumstance is endemic to college student loan collections. Since the IRS must, and does, cope with changing residence of the entire population, it could be an efficient collector. If longer terms of repayment were allowed, IRS would have even more pronounced advantages. In addition, were loan programs to include any form of income-related repayments, IRS would have to act as collector for the sake of both efficiency and privacy.

Opponents of central collections cited the evolution of residential financing as evidence that improved collection procedures accompany experience with a program. It was noted that banks, at one time, regarded long-term mortgages as unfeasible. As experience with these instruments grew, banks and other financial institutions became both more willing and more efficient in mortgage servicing. As student loan programs mature, a similar learning process would take place. Moreover, perhaps some banks or consortia of financial institutions would specialize in servicing student loans. Few barriers threaten to impede this evolution; a competitive loan market will eventually come up with a lower-cost solution. Calling on IRS is shortsighted. Even for IRS, student loan servicing will not be costless. Several questions arise: Will Congress appropriate funds for collections or will students pay these charges? If the latter, how? What kind of precedent is set by IRS collection? Does it presage a federal credit-card and billing service? What is the role of financial institutions in such a world? Until these questions can be answered satisfactorily, heavy emphasis should be given to perfecting the system that now exists. For student loans, that means servicing by financial institutions.

CONCLUSION There is no better way to summarize and characterize the conference proceedings than to report the discussion surrounding the issue of creating a National Student Loan Bank. Such an institution, in the view of most advocates, would be the simplest and most direct way to institute many of the changes in loan programs discussed at the conference. The Bank could offer lengthier repayment terms, act as an agent for dispensing subsidies for loans, introduce income-related repayments, employ the IRS as collector and colleges and universities as loan originators. Other proposals for only partially reforming loan programs, it was argued, fail to recognize the permanence of any change in social institutions: "Whatever is done now will be with us for generations." Thus, if the federal government is interested in expanding the role of loans, it should establish, from the start, the proper institutional form. The Bank advocates did not all endorse immediate implementation of every reform considered, but they argued that any institutional change should not preclude future changes in administration, loan terms, and so forth. In general, the Bank advocates at the conference were people who foresaw considerably more reliance on loans for students, whether or not they approved of such a development.

The possibility of establishing a national bank for student loans brings forth what can only be called a Jacksonian reaction from some students of higher education finance.[4] At the Brookings conference, a student loan bank was associated, first and foremost, in the minds (and words) of some participants with the elimination (or severe curtailment) of all public subsidies for higher education. All the arguments in favor of a national bank were redefined by the opposition: longer repayment period (means relieving guilt over abandoning grants for loans), more efficient collection of repayments through IRS (means enshrining loans as a major component of finance), using institutions of higher education for purpose of origination (means co-optation of the universities), maintaining a flexible charter so as to allow future refinements such as income-contingent repayments (means an overt admission that the bank is a juggernaut), and so on.

In summation, the conference discussions established that many of the reforms in student loans that were discussed *would* improve the efficiency of federal loan programs. For any specified level of loans, most of the reforms, especially if embodied in a national bank, would lead to a more economical use of public funds, to a lesser burden on borrowers, and to fewer distortions in the allocation of capital. *But the level of loans may not be independent of the efficiency of the institutional process of lending.*

---

[4] For a recent example of a wide-ranging attack on a loan bank, see Hanford and Nelson (1970, pp. 16–21).

For those who are convinced that expansion of student loans is not a potentially useful way to help students pay for college education, the present system of federal programs needs no major repairs. Some change is acceptable: Add a little stripe down the hood—it's still a Volkswagen—but a new engine might run away with the race.

References

Allen, James: statement before the Special Subcommittee on Education of the Committee on Education and Labor, House of Representatives, July 29, 1969 (to be published by the U.S. Government Printing Office, date not determined).

American Alumni Council, Council for Financial Aid to Education, and National Association of Independent Schools: *Voluntary Support of Education, 1967–68,* New York, 1969.

Arrow, Kenneth J.: *Aspects of the Theory of Risk-Bearing,* The Academic Book Store, Helsinki, 1965.

Barr, Joseph W.: in *Higher Education Amendments of 1968, Hearings before the Special Subcommittee on Education of the House Committee on Education and Labor,* 90th Cong., 2d Sess., 1968, part 1.

Becker, Gary S.: *Human Capital: A Theoretical and Empirical Analysis, with Special Reference to Education,* Columbia University Press for the National Bureau of Economic Research, 1964.

Berls, Robert H.: "Higher Education Opportunity and Achievement in the United States," in *The Economics and Financing of Higher Education in the United States,* a compendium of papers submitted to the Joint Economic Committee, 91st Cong., 1st Sess., 1969.

Bowen, Howard R.: "Financing Higher Education: Two Views (1)," *AGB Reports,* Association of Governing Boards of Universities and Colleges, vol. 10, no. 9, pp. 3–11, June, 1968.

Bowen, William G.: *The Economics of the Major Private Universities,* Carnegie Commission on Higher Education, Berkeley, 1968.

Break, George F.: "The Treatment of Lending and Borrowing in the Federal Budget," in Wilfred Lewis, Jr. (ed.), *Budget Concepts for Economic Analysis,* The Brookings Institution, 1968.

The Budget of the United States Government, Fiscal Year 1971, Government Printing Office, Washington, D.C., Appendix, 1970.

Campbell, Robert, and Barry N. Siegel: "The Demand for Higher Education in the United States 1919–1964," *American Economic Review,* vol. 57, no. 3, pp. 482–494, June, 1967.

Carnegie Commission on Higher Education: *Quality and Equality: New Levels of Federal Responsibility for Higher Education,* a special report and recommendations by the Carnegie Commission on Higher Education, McGraw-Hill Book Company, New York, 1968.

Carnegie Commission on Higher Education: *Quality and Equality: Revised Recommendations, New Levels of Federal Responsibility for Higher Education,* McGraw-Hill Book Company, New York, 1970.

Cartter, Allan M.: "The Supply and Demand for College Teachers," *Journal of Human Resources,* vol. 1, no. 1, pp. 22–38, Summer, 1966.

College Scholarship Service: *Manual for Financial Aid Officers, 1967 Edition,* College Entrance Examination Board, New York, 1967.

Congressional Record, daily edition, August 12, 1969, pp. S. 9679–9723, S. 9686–9687.

Cook, Gail C. A., and David A. A. Stager: *Student Financial Assistance Programs,* with special reference to the Province of Ontario, Institute for the Quantitative Analysis of Social and Economic Policy, University of Toronto, 1969.

Creager, John A., Alexander W. Astin, Robert F. Boruch, and Alan E. Bayer: *National Norms for Entering College Freshmen–Fall 1968,* ACE Research Reports, vol. 3, no. 1, American Council on Education, Washington, D.C., 1968.

Daniere, André: "The Benefits and Costs of Alternative Federal Programs of Financial Aid to College Students," in *The Economics and Financing of Higher Education in the United States,* a compendium of papers submitted to the Joint Economic Committee, 91st Cong., 1st Sess., 1969.

Denison, Edward F.: "Effects of Standardization Earnings Differentials by Levels of Education and Their Bearing on the 'Two-Fifths' Adjustment." (Unpublished manuscript.)

Denison, Edward F.: *The Sources of Economic Growth in the United States and the Alternatives Before Us,* Supplementary Paper no. 13, Committee for Economic Development, 1962.

Directorate for Scientific Affairs: *Educational Policy and Planning: Sweden,* OECD, Paris, 1967.

"Distribution of Gross Family Income," memorandum from Office of Education, Division of Student Financial Aid, April 10, 1968.

Duesenberry, James S.: *Money and Credit: Impact and Control,* Prentice-Hall, Inc. Englewood Cliffs, N.J., 1964.

Emergency Insured Student Loan Act of 1969, P.L. 91-95, October, 1969.

Emergency Student Loan Act of 1969, Hearing before the Subcommittee on Education of the Senate Committee on Labor and Public Welfare, 91st Cong., 1st Sess., 1969, pp. 18–42.

Federal Reserve Bulletin, vol. 56, no. 7, pp. A23, A37, A38, A55, July, 1970.

Friedman, Milton: "The Higher Schooling in America," *The Public Interest,* no. 11, Spring, 1968.

Glennerster, Howard, Stephen Merrett, and Gail Wilson: "A Graduate Tax," *Cornmarket Higher Education Review,* vol. 1, no. 1, London, Winter, 1968.

Gordon, Kermit (ed.): *Agenda for the Nation,* The Brookings Institution, 1968.

Green, Edith: Statement in *Congressional Record,* daily edition, October 16, 1969, p. H. 9649.

Hanford, George H. and James E. Nelson: "Federal Student Loan Plans: The Dangers Are Real," *College Board Review,* vol. 75, pp. 16–21, Spring, 1970.

Hansen, W. Lee, and Burton A. Weisbrod: *Benefits, Costs and Finance of Public Higher Education,* Markham Publishing Company, 1969.

The Higher Education Opportunity Act of 1970, Title IV, 91st Cong., 2d Sess., H.R. 16621. (Also S. 3636, same session.)

Kuznets, Simon: *Capital in the American Economy: Its Formation and Financing,* Princeton University Press for the National Bureau of Economic Research, 1961.

Lybrand, Ross Bros. and Montgomery: "Survey of Lender Practices Relating to the Guaranteed Student Loan Program Established by the Higher Education Act of 1965," for the U.S. Office of Education, February, 1970.

Muirhead, Peter P.: in *Higher Education Amendments of 1968, Hearings before the Special Subcommittee on Education of the House Committee on Education and Labor,* 90th Cong., 2d Sess., 1968, part 1.

Musgrave, Richard A.: *The Theory of Public Finance: A Study in Public Economy,* McGraw-Hill Book Company, New York, 1959.

"Not Enough Money to Go Around," *Business Week,* December 6, 1969, pp. 167–170.

Notes and Working Papers Concerning the Administration of Programs Authorized Under Student Financial Assistance Statutes (College Board Study), prepared for the Subcommittee on Education of the Senate Committee on Labor and Public Welfare, 90th Cong., 2d Sess., 1968.

Office of Education Appropriations for 1971, Hearings before a Subcommittee of the House Committee on Appropriations, 91st Cong., 2d Sess., 1970.

O'Neill, June: "Resource Use in Higher Education," to be published by the Carnegie Commission on Higher Education.

Panel on Educational Innovation to the U.S. Commissioner of Education, the Director of the National Science Foundation, and the Special Assistant to the President for Science and Technology: *Educational Opportunity Bank,* U.S. Government Printing Office, Washington, D.C., 1967.

Panos, Robert J., Alexander W. Astin, and John A. Creager: *National Norms for Entering College Freshmen — Fall 1967,* ACE Research Reports, vol. 2, no. 7, American Council on Education, 1967.

Pechman, Joseph A., Henry J. Aaron, and Michael K. Taussig: *Social Security: Perspectives for Reform,* The Brookings Institution, 1968.

"Percentage of Number of Students Aided," memorandum from U.S. Office of Education, Division of Student Financial Aid, April 10, 1969.

"Percentage of Total Amount by Type of Institution," memorandum from U.S. Office of Education, Division of Student Financial Aid, April 10, 1969.

President's Commission on Budget Concepts: "Problems in Implementing a Capital Budget for Loans," in Wilfred Lewis, Jr. (ed.), *Budget Concepts for Economic Analysis,* The Brookings Institution, 1968.

Rivlin, Alice M.: *The Role of the Federal Government in Financing Higher Education,* The Brookings Institution, 1961.

Saunders, H. Reed: *Handbook for Financial Aid Officers,* American College Testing Program, 1968.

Segal, David: "'Equity' Versus 'Efficiency' in Higher Education," in *The Economics and Financing of Higher Education in the United States,* a compendium of papers submitted to the Joint Economic Committee, 91st Cong., 1st Sess., 1969.

Shell, Karl: "Notes on the Educational Opportunity Bank," *National Tax Journal,* vol. 23, no. 2, pp. 214–220, June, 1970.

Shell, Karl, Franklin M. Fisher, Duncan K. Foley, and Ann F. Friedlaender, in association with James J. Behr, Jr., Stanley Fischer, and Ran D. Mosenson: "The Educational Opportunity Bank: An Economic Analysis of a Contingent Repayment Loan Program for Higher Education," *National Tax Journal,* vol. 21, no. 1, pp. 2–45, March, 1968.

Student Assistance Act of 1969, 91st Cong., 1st Sess., S. 1788, April 14, 1969.

Swedish Institute for Cultural Relations with Foreign Countries: *Fact Sheets on Sweden: State Study Assistance in Sweden,* Swedish Information Service, New York, January, 1968.

Thurow, Lester C.: "The Optimum Lifetime Distribution of Consumption Expenditures," *American Economic Review,* vol. 59, p. 329, June, 1969*a*.

Thurow, Lester C.: *Poverty and Discrimination,* The Brookings Institution, 1969*b*.

Tobin, James: "An Essay on Principles of Debt Management," in William Fellner et al., *Fiscal and Debt Management Policies,* prepared for the Commission on Money and Credit, Prentice-Hall, Inc., Englewood Cliffs, N.J., 1963.

U.S. Bureau of the Budget: *Special Analyses, Budget of the United States, Fiscal Year 1972,* U.S. Government Printing Office, Washington, D.C., 1971, p. 67.

U.S. Bureau of the Census: "School Enrollment: October 1967 and 1968," *Current Population Reports,* ser. P-20, no. 190, 1969.

U.S. Bureau of the Census: *U.S. Census of Population: 1960, Subject Reports, Occupation by Earnings and Education,* Final Report PC(2)-7B, 1963.

U.S. Department of Health, Education, and Welfare: *Budget Estimates, Fiscal Year 1970,* vol. VI. (Unpublished.)

U.S. Department of Health, Education, and Welfare: *1967 Manual of Policies and Procedures,* U.S. Office of Education, National Defense Student Loan Program, Appendix 2, 1967.

U.S. Department of Health, Education, and Welfare: *Education in the Seventies,* May, 1968.

U.S. Department of Health, Education, and Welfare: "National Education Warehouse," U.S. Office of Education memorandum, February 26, 1969*a*.

U.S. Department of Health, Education, and Welfare: *Projections of Educational Statistics to 1977–78,* 1968 ed., 1969*b*.

U.S. Department of Health, Education, and Welfare: *Toward a Long-Range Plan for Federal Financial Support for Higher Education,* A Report to the President, Office of the Assistant Secretary for Planning and Evaluation, January, 1969*c*.

U.S. **Office of Education:** *Annual Report of Repayments on National Defense Student Loans, Fiscal Year 1968.* (Unpublished.)

U.S. **Office of Education:** *Frequency of Borrowing Table,* Division of Student Financial Aid, Insured Loans Branch, 1969*a*. (Mimeographed.)

U.S. **Office of Education:** *Guaranteed Student Loan Program,* Bureau of Higher Education, Division of Student Financial Aid, Insured Loans Branch, May, 1969*b*. (Mimeographed.)

U.S. **Office of Education:** *National Defense Student Loan Program,* section B, part 1. (Unpublished.)

U.S. **Office of Education:** "NDSL Operations Summary." (Unpublished.)

Vickrey, William: "A Proposal for Student Loans," in Selma J. Mushkin (ed.), *Economics of Higher Education,* U.S. Department of Health, Education, and Welfare, 1962.

Weisbrod, Burton A., and Peter Karpoff: "Monetary Returns to College Education, Student Ability, and College Quality," *Review of Economics and Statistics,* vol. 50, no. 4, pp. 491–497, November 1968.

Wold, Ronald A.: *Alternative Methods of Federal Funding for Higher Education,* Carnegie Commission on Higher Education, Berkeley, 1968, Appendix 1d.

Appendix A: Cost Estimates for Higher Education Loans

There are no widely accepted, comprehensive measures of higher education enrollments, costs, and student charges. For the sake of familiarity and reproducibility, most of the estimates used for this report were derived from official U.S. Office of Education (OE) data, modified only when necessary. The general consensus seems to be that OE projections tend to understate enrollments, costs, and charges. Since the official numbers were not adjusted for this possibility, a similar bias exists here.

FULL COSTS To estimate full costs of higher education in 1977–78, enrollments and full cost per student were estimated separately; the product was used as the full-cost projection.

Enrollments The most relevant measure of enrollment for our purposes is called "total degree-credit enrollment" in the OE lexicon.[1] This measure includes all undergraduates working for a degree, as well as graduate students working for a degree. Excluded are those students enrolled in vocational or general studies programs. In order to distinguish between full-time and part-time enrollments, both of which are counted in degree-credit enrollment, the OE survey data were used to convert the number of part-time students into full-time equivalents (FTE). Results for the FTE projections and details are given in Table A-1.

Costs The concept of full costs discussed in the text comes closest to outlays of institutions of higher education allocable to (and po-

---

[1] For definitions, see U.S. Department of Health, Education and Welfare: *Projections of Educational Statistics to 1977–78*, 1968 Edition, Office of Education, Government Printing Office, Washington, D.C., 1969, Table 4, p. 12 (hereafter cited as HEW, 1969*b*).

TABLE A-1 *Degree-credit enrollment in U.S. institutions of higher education, by type of enroll-ment, fall, 1967, and projections for fall, 1977*

Type of enrollment	Number enrolled (thousands)		Percent change	
	Fall, 1967	*Fall, 1977*	*Total*	*Annual, 1967–77*
Full-time degree credit enrollment	4,560*	6,830	+49.8	+4.1
Part-time degree credit enrollment	1,788*	2,854	+59.6	+4.8
Full-time equivalent degree credit enrollment	5,150*	7,772	+50.9	+4.2

*Preliminary.

SOURCES: Lines 1 and 2: HEW (1969*b*, Table 8, p. 16). Line 3: line 1 plus 33 percent of line 2. This percentage is based on a 1964 survey of degree-credit enrollment in institutions of higher education by the U.S. Office of Education. See HEW (1969*b*, Table A, p. 105, footnote 37).

tentially chargeable to) degree-credit students. No OE series fully reflects this concept. To build up a measure for the 1967–68 base year, operating expenditures were estimated as follows. Cost fig-ures from OE tables on educational and general-purpose expen-ditures for 1967–68 were included for student education (general administration, instruction, libraries, plant maintenance, and so forth), and related activities (lab schools, hospitals, and so forth). Omitted were expenditures on organized research. In addition, expenditures for auxiliary enterprises and student aid (dormitories, cafeterias, scholarships) were included, but all capital outlays were deducted. To the extent that capital outlays were included in organized research, too large an amount may have been deducted from the total. Table A-2 summarizes these estimates.

TABLE A-2 *Operating expenditures for institutions of higher education by components, 1967–68, and projections for 1977–78*

Expenditure component	Expenditures	
	1967–68	
	Total (billions of dollars)	*Per full-time equivalent student (dollars)*
Student education	$ 8.8	$1,709
Related activities	0.8	155
Auxiliary enterprises and student aid	3.2	621
Less capital outlay included in above	−$ 0.6	−$ 116
TOTALS	$ 12.2	$2,369

SOURCES: Column 1: HEW (1969*b*, Table 46, p. 92); column 2: column 1 divided by FTE from Table A-1; column 3: column 2 multiplied by (1 plus column 4 com-pounded for 10 years); column 4: see text (last item is estimated).

Column 2 of Table A-2 shows the operating expenditures per FTE student from Table A-1. These cost estimates were extended to 1977–78 by assumed rates of increase for each cost line. The assumed rates of increase in cost are based on little more than guesswork. The annual rate of increase in student education per FTE student can with some confidence be expected to fall within the range of 4 percent to 7½ percent. The lower limit is the estimated annual increase in income per student in public institutions over the period 1959–1966 (HEW, 1969c, p. 46) and might be expected to come about if (a) faculty salary increases moderated from their recent annual rate of increase of about 5 percent (William Bowen, 1968, p. 28) and (b) student-faculty ratios rise somewhat and/or (c) two-year institutions increase in relative importance. The upper end of the range of possible increases is represented by Bowen's estimate of the average expected growth in student education costs for the decade 1965–1975 at major private universities (ibid., p. 33). If Bowen's estimate for major private institutions is accurate, then the rate for all institutions should be less, given the recent ability of privates to increase their expenditure relative to all other institutions (HEW, 1969c, p. 46). A 5 percent annual growth rate for student education expenditures per FTE student was selected for this study. All other costs per FTE student—for related activities, auxiliary enterprises, and capital outlays—were assumed to grow more slowly: 3 percent per year. These items are fairly representative of the consumer price index, and the special reasons

1977–78	
Per full-time equivalent student (dollars)	*Annual growth rate per full-time equivalent student, 1967–68 to 1977–78 (percent)*
$2,784	5
208	3
835	3
—$ 156	—(3)
$3,671	(4.5)

TABLE A-3 *Capital costs for institutions of higher education, by type of asset, 1967–68 (millions of dollars)*

Asset	Replacement cost of capital stock*	Adjusted replacement cost	Annual depreciation	Annual interest
Land	$ 3,613	$ 2,637		$ 132
Buildings and improvements	24,088	17,584	352	879
Equipment	3,356	2,450	123	123
TOTALS	$31,057	$22,671	$475	$1,134

*July 1, 1967.

SOURCES: Column 1: June O'Neill ("Resource Use in Higher Education," forthcoming). Column 2: 73 percent of column 1. In 1965–66, organized research represented 27 percent of operating expenditures as defined in Table A-2. See HEW (1969*b*, Table 46). Column 3: based on a 2 percent annual depreciation rate for buildings; 5 percent per annum for equipment. Column 4: based on a 5 percent interest rate on all capital assets.

for relative cost increases associated with student education (William Bowen, 1968, p. 25) do not apply to these items. The third column in Table A-2 represents estimates of operating cost per FTE in 1977.

So far, no imputation has been made for costs of capital. To derive estimates of annual cost of capital—depreciation and forgone interest—data derived by June O'Neill were employed. From Mrs. O'Neill's capital value data, we derived the total of $1.6 billion for charges against capital in 1967–68.[2] These charges represent 13 percent of operating costs, as previously defined, in that year. Full cost estimates, including capital charges, derived by assuming that capital charges would continue at 13 percent of operating cost through 1977–78, are shown in Table A-4.

TABLE A-4
Full costs of higher education in 1967–68 and projections for 1977–78

Type of cost	1967–68	1977–78
Operating (billions)	$ 12.2	$ 28.5
Capital (billions)	1.6	3.7
Full cost (billions)	$ 13.8	$ 32.2
Full cost per full-time equivalent student	$2,680	$4,143

SOURCES: Operating cost: 1967–68 from Table A-2; 1977–78 derived from Tables A-2 and A-1. Capital cost: 1967–68 from Table A-3, sum of columns 3 and 4; 1977–78 equals 13 percent of line 1 (capital costs are estimated as 13 percent of operating costs; see text). Full cost per full-time equivalent student: line 3 divided by Table A-1, line 3.

[2] The data were adjusted to eliminate charges against organized research capital. See Table A–3, column 2.

Total student charges represent the actual costs incurred by all students working for a degree. Costs per student are projected by recent trends in tuition and other charges. Thus, the estimates derived below implicitly assume state, federal, and private gift giving to grow at approximately the same rate as in the recent past. To estimate student charges, the FTE's of Table A-1 were divided into public and private institution components. For each component average tuition, room and board charges were derived as shown in Table A-5. The "total student charges" aggregates of $7.5 billion in 1967–68 and $16.8 billion in 1977–78 represent the approximate volume a loan program would have to attain in order to provide all students with enough funds to pay all charges for tuition and fees as well as room and board costs, whether or not the latter are provided to them through institutions of higher education.

STUDENT
CHARGES NET
OF FAMILY
ABILITY TO
PAY
In the loan role under discussion here, there is a wide variety of alternative formulations. It is possible to estimate current student charges by income class, and then subtract, by income class, an amount the family is thought to be able to pay. However, the institution of such a vast national loan program would more than likely affect the pattern of current student charges by income class.

Alternatively, we could estimate the total family ability to pay for the entire student population and subtract that total from the previously estimated total student charges. This estimate was computed for 1967–68 for this study and showed that, in

TABLE A-5 *Number of students enrolled in institutions of higher education and total student charges, 1967–68, and projections for 1977–78*

	1967–68		1977–78	
Number of students and type of charge	*Public*	*Private*	*Public*	*Private*
Full-time equivalent enrollment (thousands)	3,471*	1,679*	5,660*	2,112*
Tuition and required fees	$ 292†	$1,327†	$ 471‡	$2,515‡
Room and board	784§	932§	1,074¶	1,277¶
Total charge per student	$1,076	$2,259	$1,545	$3,792
Total student charges (billions)	$3.73	$3.79	$8.74	$8.01

SOURCES: *HEW (1969*b*, Table 16, p. 24. † HEW (1969*b*, Table 49, p. 99). ‡ 1960–61 to 1967–68 changes were projected to 1977–78. Assumed annual rate of increase is 4.9 percent for public schools and 6.6 percent for private schools. § HEW (1969*b*, Table 49, p. 99). ¶ Assumed to grow at 3.2 percent per annum, the mean rate of increase from 1960–61 to 1967–68.

the aggregate, parents of college-going students could afford over half a billion *more* than the total of all student charges for that year (see Table A-6). The implications of this finding are that (a) many parents are not now paying what it has been estimated they can afford and (b) a change to a strong income-discriminating system would make our previous estimates of student charges incorrect. Rather than elaborate on the dynamics of this kind of radical change in college pricing, we adopted a modest plan to serve under this standard.

In 1967–68, the average student charge per FTE student was $1,460. We assume that every student is eligible for a loan in that amount, provided he can demonstrate that his family can afford no contribution. For students whose families can afford to contribute, the maximum loan of $1,460 is reduced by the

TABLE A-6
Income distribution and student financial need, fall, 1967

Parental income	Percent of all students*	Full-time equivalent in class	Ability to pay
Less than $4,000	5.9	303,850	
$ 4,000–$5,999	11.5	592,250	$ 320
$ 6,000–$7,999	16.6	854,900	750
$ 8,000–$9,999	17.0	875,500	1,150
$10,000–$14,999	26.7	1,375,050	1,830
$15,000–$19,999	10.2	525,300	2,930
$20,000–$24,999	4.7	242,050	3,600†
$25,000–$29,999	2.5	128,750	3,600†
$30,000 and over	5.0	257,500	3,600†
TOTALS	100.0	5,150,000	

*Data pertain to fall 1967 freshmen only. Percentages are assumed to apply to the entire FTE student body in 1967–68. The percent that did not know family income were distributed proportionately.

†For families over $20,000 income, we assumed an ability to pay of $3,600, the College Scholarship Service rate for a $20,000 family.

SOURCES: Column 1: derived from Panos et al. (1967, p. 33). Column 2: column 1 times 5,150,000, the estimated FTE enrollment for the fall of 1967. Column 3: equals 1967 College Scholarship Service estimates of family contribution for 2-parent–2-children families. Entry is at midpoint of range. (Saunders, 1968, Appendix, exhibit 6, p. 2.) Column 4: the difference between the average student charge (see Table A-5), $1,460, and column 3. Column 5: column 4 times column 2. Column 6: column 2 times column 3. The sum of entries in this column is the aggregate family ability to pay referred to in the text.

family contribution. This maximum is similar to the federally insured portion of the federal Guaranteed Loan Program under which a maximum loan ($1,500) is established. However, unlike the Guaranteed Loan Program, the standard here assumes the imposition of a means test, rather than a demonstration of credit worthiness to a lending institution. The estimates presented in Table A-6 imply a 1967–68 program serving up to 2.6 million FTE students (all from families of under-$10,000 income) at an average loan of about $760 for a total loan volume of $1.9 billion.

For 1977–78, this standard would require that we estimate the impact of the interplay of the following forces: (a) growing family incomes, (b) changes in income-class composition of student bodies, and (c) changes in the standards by which parental

Gap	Cost of gap (billions of dollars)	Total family ability to pay (billions of dollars)
$1,460	$0.444	
1,140	0.675	$ .190
710	0.607	.641
310	0.271	1.007
		2.516
		1.539
		.871
		.464
		.927
	$1.997	$8.155

TABLE A-7 *Number of borrowers and number of students under standard of student charges net of family ability to pay, 1967–68, and projected charges, 1977–78*

	1967–68	Estimated annual growth rate, 1967–68 to 1977–78 (percent)	1977–78
Borrowers (number and percent growth rate)	2,626,500	4.2	3,963,651
Average loan or growth rate	$760	4.0	$1,122
Total loans (billions of dollars and growth rate)	$1.997	8.3	$4.447

SOURCES: Column 1: derived from Table A-6. Column 2: borrowers: annual growth of FTE enrollments shown in Table A-1; average loan: annual growth in total student charges per FTE enrollment shown in Table A-5; total loans derived from columns 1 and 3. Column 3: column 1 times (1 plus column 2)^{10}.

contributions are estimated.[3] Such estimates are not assumed for 1977–78 that (a) the number of eligible borrowers would grow at the same rate as FTE enrollment over the 1967–68 base period and (b) the average loan would grow at the same rate as total student charges per FTE over the base period. The estimates are shown in Table A-7.

STATUS QUO The four major federally sponsored loan programs are the National Defense Student Loan program (NDSL), the Guaranteed Student Loan Program (GLP), the Nursing Student Loan program, and the Health Professions Student Loan program. The former two are administered by the U.S. Office of Education and the latter two by the National Institutes of Health (NIH). All but the GLP are direct loans: The federal budget supplies most of the capital for the loans.[4]

For purposes of estimation and projection, we aggregated the two NIH programs, each of which is small. In Table A-8, we recorded the actual program levels for 1967–68. Approximately

[3] The last point is important. It is not realistic simply to move down a table of family contributions for 1967 in order to estimate the expected contribution at a later date when all incomes have risen. The CSS standards are based, in part, on the U.S. Bureau of Labor Statistics' "moderate level of living," out of which the contribution is quite low. The moderate income level will rise as incomes go up and, therefore, the entire College Scholarship Service schedule should shift over time. See College Scholarship Service (1967, part 5).

[4] Educational institutions provide small matching funds, and repayments are also a source of new loan volume.

1 million students were aided at an average loan of about $700.[5] For status quo projections to 1977–78, the FTE enrollment growth rate for the next decade was applied to the number of borrowers, and the total student charges growth rate was applied to the average loan.

These assumptions presuppose that the rules governing who is eligible for each program will be adjusted to make possible the projections. Projections computed for each of the three programs separately, are shown in Table A-8.

TABLE A-8 *Projections of loans to students of higher education in fiscal year 1978 if the fiscal year 1968 status quo were maintained, by loan programs*

Loan program	Fiscal year 1968	Estimated annual growth rate, 1967–68 to 1977–78 (percent)	1977–78
National Defense Student Loans			
Loan volume (millions)	$ 234		$ 521
Number of borrowers and growth rate	429,000	4.2	647,404
Average loan and growth rate	$ 545	4.0	$ 804
Guaranteed Loans			
Loan volume (millions)	$ 436		$ 971
Number of borrowers and growth rate	515,408	4.2	777,802
Average loan and growth rate	$ 846	4.0	$1,249
Nursing and Health Professions Student Loans			
Loan volume (millions)	$ 43		$ 96
Number of borrowers and growth rate	47,787	4.2	72,115
Average loan and growth rate	$ 900	4.0	$1,328
Total volume (millions)	$ 713		$1,588
Total borrowers	992,195		1,497,321
Average loan	$ 719		$1,061

SOURCES: *The Budget of the United States Government, Fiscal Year 1970* and supporting documents. For growth assumptions, see Table A-7.

[5] The total number of student borrowers overstates the coverage of the programs for two reasons. First, some students borrow from more than one program in a given year: Such students are counted more than once in these tables. Second, eligibility in the Guaranteed Loan Program extends to students in technical schools not covered in our FTE enrollment estimates. Thus, the estimated one million borrowers is not strictly comparable to our enrollment estimates.

Under the accessory-aid standard, loans would be available to freshmen and sophomores for charges in excess of those at two-year public colleges and for the entire student charges of later years of higher education.

To estimate loan volume in 1967–68 under this standard, we first computed the full-time equivalent number of freshmen and sophomores. This total came to 58 percent of FTE enrollment, or 2,987,000 students, in 1967–68.[6]

Then the charges for tuition and room and board at two-year public institutions were derived from OE data. These charges amounted to $744 (HEW, 1969*b*, p. 96) in 1967–68. Total freshman plus sophomore charges at the two-year public rate thus amounted to $2.2 billion. This would be the cost of some minimum basic federal or state plan to subsidize the first two years of college (or at least the student charge fraction thereof). Total student charges for 1967–68 were $7.5 billion as indicated in Table A-5. Thus, a loan plan would have to be able to support about $5.3 billion in loans under the accessory-aid standard. All students except freshmen and sophomores at two-year public

---

[6] Unfortunately the OE does not report data for students in the first two years of college. The OE series "first time degree credit enrollment" is closely related to "freshmen" but the estimates for this series in the period 1965–1967 are erratic. The reason for the erratic behavior is that the series is based on the number of 18-year-olds in a given school year—and births bulged in 1947–48. The birth-related estimates are revised on the basis of fall surveys, but the 1966 and 1967 data which were needed for our purposes were not available when the estimates were made. Freshman and sophomore enrollment was, therefore, derived as follows: Undergraduate enrollment in fall of 1967–68, E_t, is defined as:
$$E_t = F_t + d_1 F_{t-1} + d_2 F_{t-2} + d_3 F_{t-3}$$
where F_t = Freshman in fall of 1967, d_1 = Fraction of all F_{t-1} who are enrolled in fall of 1967, and so forth.

Let $F_t = (1 + r) F_{t-1}$ for all t where r is the rate of growth of freshmen classes assumed constant over t to $t-3$.
Then $E_t = F_t [1 + d_1/(1 + r) + d_2/(1 + r)^2 + d_3/(1 + r)^3]$ and $F_t = (1 + r)^3/[(1 + r)^3 + d_1(1 + r)^2 + d_2(1 + r) + d_3]$

Using $r = 0.055$ (estimated from first-time enrollees 1964–67 in HEW [1969*b*, p. 13]) and retention rates of $d_1 = 0.75$, $d_2 = 0.60$, $d_3 = 0.51$ (derived from Berls [1969, p. 163]) results in an estimate of $F_t/E_t = 0.37$. This is our estimate of the fraction of all undergraduates who are freshmen. The sophomore fraction estimate is given by $d_1 F_{t-1}/E_t = d_1/(1 + r) = 0.26$. Thus, we estimate that freshmen and sophomores represent about 63 percent of all undergraduates. Undergraduate full-time equivalents in 1967–68 represent only 92 percent of all FTE enrollment (derived from HEW [1969*b*, p. 21]). Hence,

institutions would be eligible for this plan.[7] We estimate the FTE eligible enrollment at two-year public institutions at 669,000, leaving 4,481,000 eligible recipients of loans.[8]

For 1977–78, we assumed that the same ratio of accessory aid to total student charges as prevailed in 1967–68 would prevail in the later year. Thus, 1977–78 accessory aid would equal 5.3/7.5 $\times$ $16.8 billion = $11.87 billion. Assuming that eligible borrowers grow at the same rate as FTE enrollments results in an eligible borrowership of 6.8 million, or about $1,746 per FTE borrower.

we estimate freshmen and sophomores at 58 percent (0.63 times 0.92) of total FTE enrollment.

[7] We are assuming here that two-year public colleges have the lowest student charges of all institutions.

[8] According to HEW (1969*b*, Table 10, p. 18), FTE at *all* two-year institutions aggregated 777,000 in 1967–68. Over 10 percent of these were at private two-year colleges.

Appendix B: Subsidies in Federal Loan Programs

The meaning of the word *subsidy* in federal loan programs is subject to wide variations in interpretation. In order to clarify the use of the term in this report, and the alternative possibilities, this section has been prepared. For illustrative purposes, program provisions and credit market conditions as they existed in 1968–69 are used.

ABSENCE OF GOVERNMENT PROGRAMS Suppose first that no government direct or guarantee programs existed in 1968–69. Some students would have been able to borrow from lending agencies during this period at varying rates depending on geography, credit standing of the family, and so forth. One of the lower rates available during this period was the rate charged at federal employees' credit unions: these ranged from 9 percent to 12 percent, depending on the nature of the collateral, and from 5- to 10-year repayment cycles. These loans were not guaranteed by the federal program. Thus, in the absence of government programs, student loan interest rates would have been, say, 10 percent, and this rate can be interpreted as the "unsubsidized" interest rate.

GUARANTEES During 1968–69, the GLP provided loans on the following terms. (Some of the rules governing this program changed in midyear. The description fits the latter half of the year.) Federal (or state or nonprofit private) guarantees were provided on loans to students if, at the institution of the repayment period, the repayment schedule did not exceed 7 percent interest, all paid by the borrowers. During the period of enrollment, military service, and other exempt periods, the federal government paid lenders interest at no more than 7 percent. Thus, in most cases, the existence of the guarantee provision lowered the return to the lender to 7 percent. In one sense, then, 7 percent represents a subsidized rate. The difference between

10 percent and 7 percent is the value to the lender of the reduction in risk associated with the guarantee of the loan.

From another perspective, however, it is misleading to refer to 7 percent as a subsidized rate. A major purpose of the guarantee is to remove an imperfection in the capital market—that is, to compensate for the inability of the lender to repossess the capital financed by the loan—and to make lenders respond to risks as they really are from a social point of view. Looked at this way, 7 percent interest is what the market rate would be if the market were operating perfectly, and in this sense 7 percent can be called an unsubsidized interest rate. (Unfortunately, it cannot really be asserted that 7 percent was the equilibrium market rate given the guarantee, because 7 percent was the ceiling set by legislation, and, as indicated in Chapter 4, this rate failed to clear the market.) This is the practice used in this study. The market rate (to lenders) in guaranteed loans is considered the dividing line for subsidies.

The interest rate to the borrower in 1968–69 was not 7 percent. As far as the borrower is concerned, he receives an interest-free loan during the enrollment and military periods. It is only when his repayment cycle commences that he is charged 7 percent interest on the loan principal. Thus, the true interest cost to a student participating in the GLP in 1968–69 was somewhere between 0 percent (if he paid back the loan before the first repayment fell due) and about 7 percent (if he borrowed "the day before he graduated"). Under reasonable assumptions—3 years of enrollment-military service, 10-year repayment cycle after that—the "7 percent" guaranteed loan costs the student 4.25 percent. That is, if at the point in time that a $1,000 loan was granted, the student put $1,000 in a savings account paying about 4.25 percent, his account would exactly have paid off the guaranteed loan. The difference between 4.25 percent and 7 percent represents the subsidy to the student under the GLP, and it is entirely attributable to the fact that the government pays the interest during enrollment.[1]

---

[1] The illustrations assume that all payments are made annually, the first payment due four years from the time the loan originates and the last payment thirteen years from that date. No interest is paid by the student for three years. Since both federal programs allow about a one year interest-free grace period after student status lapses, we are implicitly assuming that the average borrower has two full years of school ahead of him.

A survey conducted by Lybrand, Ross Bros. and Montgomery for the U.S. Office of Education (1970) indicates that 54 percent of the students receiving guaranteed loans are in their first two years of postsecondary education (p.

DIRECT LOANS The NDSL program in 1968–69 offered student loans that required no repayment during enrollment, military, and certain other periods, and a 3 percent rate during repayment. Once again, these "3 percent loans" cost the student less than 3 percent, since the interest cost is zero during the exempt periods. Assuming as above that the student maintains enrollment or other exempt status for 3 years and repays the loan over a 10-year cycle, the true annual interest cost of this loan to the borrower is about 1⅞ percent. Thus, the subsidy (ignoring teacher cancellations) on NDEA loans is represented by the difference between 7 percent and 1⅞ percent. This subsidy is larger than that of the GLP solely because of the lower rate employed for repayment schedules in NDSL; both programs yield the same subsidy during enrollment.

DOLLAR VALUES OF SUBSIDIES Because it is difficult to conceptualize the meaning of differences in interest rates, these subsidy estimates have been converted into dollars in the text. The technique for these conversions is as follows. For each program (using the enrollment period and repayment terms assumed above) we identify the stream of repayments to be made on a $1,000 loan. That stream of repayments is discounted back to the time the loan was initiated to give the *present value of repayments*. The difference between the present value of repayments and the principal value of the loan is the (dollar value of) the subsidy. Another name for the present value of repayments is the *principal value of a loan made at the discount rate used in the calculation* or, briefly, pure loan.

It is clear that the appropriate rate to use for discounting is whatever is decided upon as the *unsubsidized interest rate*. For example, if 7 percent is the *unsubsidized rate* (as used above), the calculations just described would result in a zero subsidy for any loan with a true repayment schedule of 7 percent. (The loan would be wholly a pure, or unsubsidized, loan.) For repayment schedules below 7 percent, a dollar subsidy would result.

D-34). Similarly, Office of Education data for fiscal 1968 ("National Defense Student Loan Program," Section B, part 1, unpublished) indicate that 53 percent of the borrowers in the NDSL program were freshmen or sophomores. Thus, the assumption of a three-year period in which no interest is paid by the average borrower seems reasonable.

On the other hand, the Lybrand, Ross survey indicates an expected repayment period of considerably less than 10 years (pp. D-27 and D-28). Thus, the subsidies calculated in this study should be understood as potential subsidies if the maximum repayment period were allowed.

The dollar values of subsidies and pure loans for the two federal programs in 1968–69 are indicated in Table B-1. This table should be interpreted as follows. A $1,000 Guaranteed Loan issued in 1968–69 was a combination, at the time of issue, of a gift of $184 (from the government) and an unsubsidized (7 percent) loan of $816. The gift, in the form of no interest to the borrower, accrued during enrollment. The NDSL of $1,000 consisted of $672 of unsubsidized (7 percent) loan, the present value of the enrollment-period gift of $184 and the present value of the low-interest–repayment-schedule gift of $144. The total interest subsidy in the NDSL program was thus $328 per $1,000 loan. Delaying repayments one extra year raises the interest subsidy in the NDSL program to $372 per $1,000 and in the GLP to $237 per $1,000.

In 1967–68, both programs involved no interest during enrollment and a 3 percent rate during the repayment period. The interest ceiling during this period was 6 percent. Using the assumptions of Table B-1, the implicit interest subsidies in both programs were $275.56 per $1,000 loan. The remaining $724.44 was a pure (6 percent) loan.

GOVERNMENT BORROWING COSTS AS DISCOUNT RATE

Estimates on loan subsidies similar to those presented in this chapter have been made by others, using most typically the U.S. Treasury borrowing rate to discount future payment or repayment streams.[2] The implication of such a procedure is that a student loan carrying a true interest charge to the borrower equal to the U.S. Treasury borrowing rate should be adjudged an unsubsidized or pure loan. By contrast, we have imputed subsidies to any loan carrying a true interest charge less than the market rate for Guaran-

TABLE B-1 *Pure loan and subsidy components in a $1,000 National Defense Student Loan or Guaranteed Loan, 1968–69**

| | | Present value of dollar subsidy | |
Program	Amount that is pure loan	Attributable to enrollment subsidy	Attributable to low interest during payback
Guaranteed Loan	$816.30	$183.70	
National Defense Student Loan	$672.11	$183.70	$144.19

*Assumes a 7 percent discount rate, a 3-year enrollment period, and a 10-year repayment schedule.

[2] President's Commission on Budget Concepts (1968, pp. 37–57); Barr (1968, p. 67ff).

teed Student Loans of 7 percent. Assuming that the guaranteed market interest rate exceeds the U.S. Treasury rate, the procedure used here imputes larger subsidy amounts than would the use of the U.S. Treasury rate.

To appreciate the difference between our procedure and the alternative, consider an example where the Guaranteed Loan market rate (to the lender) is 7 percent and the average current U.S. Treasury borrowing cost is 5 percent. Suppose the borrower's cost were 6 percent. Our procedure would impute a 1 percentage point subsidy to a loan granted in this period, while the alternative would treat such a loan as unsubsidized. If the loan were direct, at least some practitioners would count the 1 percentage point difference between 6 and 5 percent as a negative subsidy or a tax.

The reasonableness of either procedure depends on what accounts for the difference between the Guaranteed Loan market rate and the U.S. Treasury borrowing cost. A number of reasons could be adduced for the difference between the two rates, among which the most relevant are:

1 The Guaranteed Loan may extend for a longer term than the average federal debt, and long term debt usually carries higher interest charges.

2 The Guaranteed Loan may not be as liquid as government debt of comparable term, and this lack of convertibility into cash requires a yield premium.

3 The origination and collection costs of a Guaranteed Loan may exceed similar costs for federal securities and, thus, may require a higher yield as compensation.

Indeed, a federally insured loan is equal to a U.S. Treasury bond only in terms of risk of default; all other aspects of the loan guarantee are different.[3] The differences listed above have two things in common: they are all real costs of student loans and they all confer benefits to borrowers. The two percentage points difference between the guarantee rate and the U.S. Treasury rate is a payment to lenders for bearing greater capital-loss risks, for holding less liquid assets, and for greater holding costs. Any student-borrower

---

[3] This is strictly true only of the federal insurance part of the GLP. Many state-guaranteed loans offer guarantees of as little as 80 percent, thus imposing a 20 percent co-insurance factor on the lender.

who does pay less than 7 percent is receiving some of these services free— and he is subsidized. Even if the student borrows from
the government under the NDSL program, he is issuing an IOU
with all the attributes listed above, and unless he pays 7 percent
for the privilege, he is getting a subsidy. Either the federal government or its agents, the colleges, are absorbing the real costs listed
above. Thus, when a private-market loan exists with provisions
similar to those for direct loans, the appropriate dividing line for
subsidies should be the private-market rate. This rate should be
used to discount costs and returns for both the private and the
direct loan programs. The U.S. Treasury borrowing rate is appropriate only if there is some evidence that the loans in question would
be viewed by the private market as having the same qualities as
the average U.S. Treasury debt.

Appendix C: Basic Data

Presented in this appendix in tabular form are the data that were used as the basis of the discussion in Chapter 5 of the distribution of benefits of federal loan programs.

To estimate the incidence of benefits from the Guaranteed Loan Program (GLP), data were available from a large sample (in fact, the universe) of loans on hand in late 1968. These loans could not be broken into fiscal- or academic-year categories. However, tabulations were available (for borrowers and loan volume) for both the federally insured and state-guaranteed programs. The distribution of borrowers in these programs differs significantly, with the former being more pro-poor. The reason for this is probably that the federally insured program is more active in low-income states and is more likely to serve students in vocational schools. In Table C-1, the distribution of borrowers and of loan volume for 1967–68 and 1968–69 have been estimated by assuming that in each year the distributions in both the federal- and state-guarantee programs are the same as shown in later 1968 tabulations. Federal and total state-guarantee activities were applied as weights to these separate distributions. Since the federal program grew faster than the state-guarantee program, the weighted distribution of GLP loans is more pro-poor in 1968–69 than in the previous year. The distribution of borrowers and of dollar loan volume was tabulated only on an "adjusted family income" basis. "Adjusted family income" differs from gross income in that the former excludes 10 percent of gross income and excludes $600 for each family member. In Tables C-2 and C-3 the distribution data are converted to a gross-income basis by assuming an average family size of four in each adjusted-family-income category.

National Defense Student Loan (NDSL) distribution data are available only on a borrower basis. It is not possible to determine

TABLE C-1
*Distribution
of borrowers
and volume of
federally
insured and
state-guaranteed
loans under the
Guaranteed
Loan Program,
by adjusted-
family-income
classes,
1967–68 and
1968–69*

Type of borrower or loan volume	$0–$2,999	$3,000–$5,999	$6,000–$7,499
Percentage distribution			
Borrowers			
1. Federally insured[c]	31.0	27.7	12.0
2. State-guaranteed[d]	15.0	21.4	12.6
Loan volume			
3. Federally insured[c]	29.6	27.3	12.1
4. State-guaranteed[d]	13.7	20.0	12.3
Number of borrowers			
1967–68			
5. Federally insured[e]	25,549	22,883	9,898
6. State-guaranteed[f]	64,756	92,545	54,670
7. TOTAL	90,305	115,428	64,568
1968–69			
8. Federally insured[g]	76,749	68,739	29,732
9. State-guaranteed[g]	80,618	115,215	68,062
10. TOTAL	157,367	183,954	97,794
Loan volume (millions of dollars)			
1967–68			
11. Federally insured[h]	19.72	18.20	8.07
12. State-guaranteed[i]	50.63	73.75	45.24
13. TOTAL	70.35	91.95	53.31
1968–69			
14. Federally insured[j]	64.59	59.60	26.42
15. State-guaranteed[j]	64.30	93.66	57.45
16. TOTAL	128.89	153.26	83.87

[a] Adjusted family income is defined as 90 percent of gross income minus $600 for each family member.

[b] Details may not add to total because of rounding.

[c] Derived from a summary of 45,800 federally insured loans processed by the U.S. Department of Health, Education, and Welfare, Office of Education, as of October 16, 1968, and provided in mimeographed form by the Systems Operation Section of the Insured Loans Branch.

[d] Derived from a summary of 600,496 state-guaranteed loans processed by the U.S. Office of Education as of December 7, 1968, and provided in mimeographed form by the Systems Operation Section of the Insured Loans Branch.

[e] Row 1 times the total number of federally insured borrowers in 1967–68 divided by 100. The total number of borrowers is the number of loans presented in the fiscal 1970 budget justification data, U.S. Department of Health, Education, and Welfare

Adjusted family-income class[a]				
$7,500– $8,999	$ 9,000– $11,999	$12,000– $14,999	$15,000 and over	*Total*[b]
9.8	13.1	5.0	1.4	100.00
12.7	23.1	14.1	1.1	100.00
10.1	13.7	5.5	1.7	100.00
12.8	24.3	15.7	1.3	100.00
8,106	10,830	4,103	1,172	82,549
54,930	99,990	61,033	4,848	432,859
63,036	110,820	65,136	6,020	515,408
24,351	32,535	12,324	3,521	247,977
68,385	124,484	75,984	6,036	538,892
92,736	157,019	88,308	9,557	786,869
6.71	9.12	3.65	1.10	66.55
47.20	89.85	57.87	4.76	369.29
53.91	98.97	61.52	5.86	435.85
21.97	29.87	11.95	3.60	218.00
59.94	114.11	73.49	6.05	469.00
081.91	143.98	85.44	9.65	687.00

(Budget Estimates, Fiscal Year 1970, vol. VI, pp. 74–77). The number of loans is assumed to be equivalent to the number of borrowers.

[f] Row 2 times the total number of state-guaranteed borrowers in 1967–68 divided by 100. The number of borrowers is estimated as in row 5.

[g] The procedure is the same as in rows 5 and 6, using 1968–69 estimates of total number of borrowers, obtained in an interview with David Bayer, U.S. Office of Education, Insured Loans Branch, December, 1969.

[h] Row 3 times the total annual loan volume divided by 100. The total annual loan volume is from fiscal 1970 budget justification data (see footnote e).

[i] Row 4 times the total annual loan volume, divided by 100. The total annual loan volume is from fiscal 1970 budget justification data (see footnote e).

[j] The procedure is the same as in rows 11 and 12. Total loan volume is from interview with David Bayer (see footnote f).

TABLE C-2 *Percentage distribution of Guaranteed Loan Program borrowers, by adjusted-family-income and gross-income classes, 1967–68 and 1968–69*

Income class	Adjusted-family-income basis		Gross-income basis‡	
	1967–68*	1968–69†	1967–68	1968–69
$ 0–$2,999	17.5%	20.0%	8.8%	10.0%
$ 3,000–$5,999	22.4	23.4	8.8	10.0
$ 6,000–$7,499	12.5	12.4	10.1	10.5
$ 7,500–$8,999	12.2	11.8	10.1	10.5
$ 9,000–$11,999	21.5	20.0	22.1	21.9
$12,000–$14,999	12.6	11.2	19.9	18.7
$15,000 and over	1.2	1.2	20.3	18.4
TOTALS	100.0%	100.0%	100.0%	100.0%

*From Table C-1, row 7.

†From Table C-1, row 10.

‡Distributions of borrowers by gross-income class are derived from the distributions of borrowers by adjusted-family-income class as follows. Adjusted family income is defined on the student application for federally insured loan form as: $A = 0.9G - \$600E$ where $A =$ adjusted family income, $G =$ gross income, and $E =$ number of exemptions. By assuming that the number of exemptions equals 4 for all families, the adjusted-family-income categories were converted into gross-income categories. The distribution of borrowers by the gross-income categories shown in this table was derived by linear interpolation on these estimated gross-income breaks.

TABLE C-3 *Percentage distribution of Guaranteed Loan Program annual loan volume, by adjusted-family-income and gross-income classes, 1967–68 and 1968–69*

Income class	Adjusted-family-income basis		Gross-income basis‡	
	1967–68*	1968–69†	1967–68	1968–69
$ 0–$2,999	16.1%	18.8%	8.1%	9.4%
$ 3,000–$5,999	21.1	22.3	8.1	9.4
$ 6,000–$7,499	12.2	12.2	9.5	10.0
$ 7,500–8,999	12.4	11.9	9.5	10.0
$ 9,000–$11,999	22.7	21.0	21.8	21.6
$12,000–$14,999	14.1	12.4	20.8	19.4
$15,000 and over	1.3	1.4	22.3	20.1
TOTAL	100.0%	100.0%	100.0%	100.0%

*From Table C-1, row 13.

†From Table C-1, row 16.

‡See last footnote, Table C-2.

TABLE C-4 Distribution of borrowers, families with dependents aged 18–24, college enrollees, and nonborrowers, 1967–68

Gross-income class	Number of Guaranteed Loan Program borrowers	Number of National Defense Student Loan borrowers	Percentage distribution of National Defense Student Loan borrowers	Percentage distribution of borrowers in both programs	Percentage distribution of families with dependents aged 18–24, October, 1967	Percentage distribution of freshmen college students, fall 1967	Actual full-time equivalent enrollment	Actual full-time equivalent enrollment minus all borrowers	Percentage distribution of nonborrowers
$ 0–$2,999	45,150	97,189	22.4	15.0	10.6	4.4	226,600	84,261	2.0
$ 3,000–$5,999	45,150	120,575	27.8	17.5	23.0	13.0	669,500	503,775	12.0
$ 6,000–$7,499	51,953	69,442	16.0	12.8	13.0	12.5	643,750	522,355	12.4
$ 7,500–$8,999	51,953	56,893	13.1	11.5	11.7	12.7	654,050	545,204	12.9
$ 9,000–$11,999	113,957	59,861	13.8	18.3	16.6	19.2	988,800	814,982	19.4
$12,000–$14,999	102,772	21,683	5.0	13.1	13.1	16.0	824,000	699,545	16.6
$15,000 and over	104,473	8,445	2.0	11.9	11.9	22.4	1,153,600	1,040,682	24.7
TOTAL	515,408	434,088	100.0	100.0	100.0	100.0	5,150,000	4,210,804	100.0

SOURCES: Number of Guaranteed Loan Program borrowers: derived from Table C-2, column 3, and data on the total number of borrowers in 1967–68 in U.S. Department of Health, Education, and Welfare (*Budget Estimates, Fiscal Year 1970*, vol. VI, p. 77–63). Number of National Defense Student Loan borrowers: tabulation for fiscal year 1968 from U.S. Office of Education ("National Defense Student Loan Program," section B, part 2, line F). Families with dependents aged 18–24: derived from U.S. Bureau of the Census (1969, p. 57). Freshman college students: derived from Panos et al. (1967, p. 33). Full-time equivalent enrollment: derived from total full-time enrollment (see Appendix A), and distribution of freshman enrollment in this table.

	Annual loan volume 1967–68	Interest subsidy 1967–68	Annual loan volume 1968–69	Interest subsidy 1968–69
TABLE C-5 Annual volume and interest subsidies in National Defense Student Loan and Guaranteed Loan programs, 1967–68 and 1968–69 (millions of dollars)				
National Defense Student Loans	(1)	(2)	(3)	(4)
$ 0–$ 2,999	$ 52.92	$ 14.58	$ 59.36	$19.46
$ 3,000–$ 5,999	65.65	18.09	73.64	24.15
$ 6,000–$ 7,499	37.81	10.42	42.42	13.91
$ 7,500–$ 8,999	30.98	8.54	34.75	11.39
$ 9,000–$11,999	32.59	8.98	36.56	11.99
$12,000–$14,999	11.82	3.26	13.26	4.35
$15,000 and over	4.61	1.27	5.17	1.70
TOTAL	$236.34	$65.14	$265.10	$86.94
Guaranteed Loans	(5)	(6)	(7)	(8)
$ 0–$ 2,999	$ 35.17	$ 9.69	$ 64.44	$ 11.84
$ 3,000–$ 5,999	35.17	9.69	64.44	11.84
$ 6,000–$ 7,499	41.36	11.40	68.97	12.67
$ 7,500–$ 8,999	41.36	11.40	68.97	12.67
$ 9,000–$11,999	94.84	26.14	148.39	27.26
$12,000–$14,999	90.83	25.03	133.55	24.53
$15,000 and over	97.02	25.13	138.29	23.64
TOTAL	$435.85	$118.51	$686.98	$124.43
Total	(9)	(10)	(11)	(12)
$ 0–$ 2,999	$ 88.09	$ 24.27	$123.80	$ 31.30
$ 3,000–$ 5,999	100.82	27.78	138.08	35.99
$ 6,000–$ 7,499	79.17	21.82	111.39	26.58
$ 7,500–$ 8,999	72.34	19.94	103.72	24.06
$ 9,000–$11,999	127.43	35.12	184.95	39.25
$12,000–$14,999	102.65	28.29	146.81	28.88
$15,000 and over	101.63	26.40	143.46	25.34
TOTAL	$672.19	$183.65	$952.08	$211.37

SOURCES: *National Defense Student Loans data:* Column 1: Appendix Table C-4, column 3, times total NDSL loan volume divided by 100. NDSL tabulation for fiscal year 1968, U.S. Office of Education ("National Defense Student Loan Program," section B, part 1, line F). Column 2: column 1 times 0.2756, the present value of the subsidy on a $1 loan repayable at 3 percent in constant annual amounts from years 4 through 13 when the market interest rate is 6 percent. See Appendix B. Column 3: Appendix Table C-4, column 3, times total NDSL loan volume for 1968–69, divided by 100. Total NDSL loan volume for 1968–69 is from U.S. Department of Health, Education, and Welfare (*Budget Estimates, Fiscal Year 1970,* p. 70–77). Column 4: column 3 times 0.3279. This subsidy rate is derived

dollar loan volume by income class. Moreover, the distribution of borrowers was not available for 1968–69. Table C-4 reports the number of NDSL borrowers by gross-income classes in 1967–68. This distribution of NDSL's was used in Tables C-4 and C-5 to estimate both borrower and loan volume distributions for 1967–68 and 1968–69. It should be noted that the NDSL borrower distribution has not, in the past, changed significantly from one year to the next. The annual loan volume for GLP for the two periods also appears in Table C-5.

In addition, Table C-5 presents estimates of the (interest) subsidies implicit in both programs. The technique used was to apply to the dollar loan volume a subsidy ratio representing that fraction of the total loan which is a subsidy. The estimation of the subsidy ratios is discussed in Appendix B.

---

in Appendix Table B-1. *Guaranteed Loan Program data:* Column 5: Appendix Table C-3, next-to-last column, times 1967–68 aggregate GLP loan volume, divided by 100. Aggregate GLP loan volume from same source as NDSL loan volume for 1968–69. Column 6: column 5 times 0.2756. See column 2 for explanation of subsidy rate. The subsidy in the highest income class was reduced by (0.2756) times the $5.84 million of loans that were ineligible for interest subsidy because borrowers' adjusted family income exceeded $15,000. Column 7: Appendix Table C-3, last column, times 1968–69 total GLP loan volume divided by 100. Total 1968–69 loan volume from interview with David Bayer, U.S. Office of Education, Insured Loans Branch, December 1969. Column 8: column 7 times 0.1837. The subsidy rate is derived in Appendix Table B-1. The subsidy in the highest income class was reduced by (0.1837) times the $9.6 million of loans that were ineligible for interest subsidy because borrowers' adjusted family income exceeded $15,000.

Appendix D: A Model for Evaluating the Distribution of Benefits of Student Loans

The additional welfare from student loan programs in any income class i may be defined as:

$$W_i = U_i\, B_i \tag{1}$$

where B_i is the number of borrowers in income class i and U_i is the average increase in welfare of a borrower in income class i. Then the distribution of welfare benefits produced by student loan programs is given by:

$$\frac{W_i}{\overline{W}} = U_i\, \frac{B_i}{\overline{B}}\, \frac{\overline{B}}{\overline{W}} \qquad \text{for all } i \tag{2}$$

where $\overline{W}$, $\overline{B}$ are total welfare benefits and total borrowers, respectively. Equation 2 shows the fraction of total benefits $\overline{W}$ accruing to income class i. $\overline{B}/\overline{W}$, the last term, is a constant over all income classes. It does not affect the distribution of welfare across income classes, and $\overline{B}/\overline{W}$ can be set so that the $\Sigma_i[W_i/\overline{W}]$ = 100.

The hypothesis here is that U_i, the average increase in well-being accruing to the borrowers in income class i, is determined by:

$$U_i = a_i\, \frac{V_i}{B_i} + c_i\, \frac{S_i}{B_i} \tag{3}$$

where V_i is the dollar value of loans in income class i and S_i is the dollar value of implicit subsidies in income class i, then a_i, c_i are partial welfare coefficients (these coefficients show the welfare impact of a \$1 change in V_i/B_i and S_i/B_i, respectively, assuming that the other variable is held constant).

According to equation 3, the borrower's increase in welfare from student loans depends on the size of his loan (V_i/B_i is the average size of loan income class i) and on the size of the implicit subsidy he receives from his loan. (S_i/B_i is the average subsidy for all borrowers in class i.) This general equation is assumed to hold whether the borrower takes his benefit in the form of enrolling when he otherwise would not, or in greater higher education expenditure, or in greater noneducation consumption for the student or his family.

To simplify the following discussion, S_i is defined such that

$$S_i = s_i \, V_i \tag{4}$$

where s_i is the rate of subsidy of loans in income class i (this shows, per dollar of loan, the fraction that is subsidized).

Combining equations 2, 3, and 4 gives

$$\frac{W_i}{W} = K \frac{B_i}{\overline{B}} \, (a_i + c_i s_i) \, \frac{V_i}{B_i} \tag{5}$$

where K is an arbitrary constant.

$B_i/\overline{B}$, s_i, and V_i/B_i are observable quantities. Table D–1 presents estimates of these variables using 1968–69 data. The assumptions going into the table are many, including one that each National Defense Student Loan (NDSL) borrower borrows the average for all NDSL borrowers. This colors the results significantly. Because of the many assumptions, the table should be taken as suggestive only.

The data show that the subsidy rate declines slowly as income rises — reflecting the lesser concentration of the more highly subsidized NDSL program in higher income classes. The average loan, however, rises as we move up the income scale, for two reasons. One is the greater concentration of loans under the Guaranteed Loan Program (GLP), which average more than NDSL loans, in the high income groups. Second is the fact that the average loan within the GLP rises at higher incomes.

With the model specified and the data described, values of a_i and c_i may be selected and implications drawn. Two possible sets of values of a_i and c_i that seem plausible are discussed here:

Case I: $a_i = 0$ for all i; $c_i = 2$ for all i.

TABLE D-1 *Distribution of borrowers, amount borrowed, and rate and value of subsidy, by income class, students with loans in 1968–69*

Gross-income class (dollars)	Distribution of borrowers $B_i/\bar{B}$ (percent)	Rate of subsidy s_i (percent)	Average amount borrowed V_i/B_i (dollars)	Average value of subsidy S_i/B_i (dollars)
$ 0–$ 2,999	14.5%	0.25%	$697	$174
$ 3,000–$ 5,999	16.4	0.26	685	178
$ 6,000–$ 7,499	12.5	0.24	726	174
$ 7,500–$ 8,999	11.4	0.23	738	170
$ 9,000–$11,999	19.0	0.21	798	167
$12,000–$14,999	13.8	0.20	867	173
$15,000 and over	12.5	0.18	934	168

SOURCES: *Column 1:* Distribution of borrowers by income class, from Table 11, for NDSL, and Table C-2, for GLP, applied to 1968–69 totals of 787,000 GLP borrowers and 442,000 NDSL borrowers (Table 7). *Column 2:* Appendix Table C-5, column 12, divided by column 11. *Column 3:* Loan volume by income class, from Appendix Table C-5, column 11. Borrowers as in column 1. *Column 4:* column 2 times column 3: s_i $V_i/B_i = S_i/B_i$.

In any income class c_i should exceed a_i, since a_i is the (private) welfare weight attached to $1 of loan, while c_i is the weight attached to $1 of subsidy. An extreme case of this inequality is when $a_i = 0$ for all income classes. This means that the pure loan aspect of the GLP and NDSL does not matter; all that counts is the subsidy. (Students borrow, but only because a loan is the passkey to the subsidy.) From equation 5, it is clear that the distribution of benefits will equal the distribution of borrowers times the distribution of average subsidy per borrower. But as column 4 of Table D-1 shows, the average subsidy in 1968–69 hardly differed among income classes. The higher subsidy *rate* for the low income groups was offset by their lower average size of loan. Thus this case will result in a distribution minutely different from the $B_i/\bar{B}$ column.

Case II: $a_i = 1$ for all i; $c_i = 2$ for all i.

Here the original assumption is relaxed somewhat, and the pure-loan aspect of loans is given some weight in the individual's welfare function. A higher weight for the subsidy values implicit in the loans is retained, however.

In this case, the distribution of benefits will be less pro-poor than the previous one. The reason for this result is that the average loan rises as income goes up, and it is the average loan that is weighted by a_i.

This framework can be extended to allow the a_i and c_i to vary from one income class to another, and then social welfare weights can be applied to the results.

Appendix E: Participants in Conference on Student Loans, April 8 and 9, 1970, The Brookings Institution Economic Studies Program

Henry J. Aaron
The Brookings Institution

Robert Abate
American National Bank, Chicago

F. E. Balderston
University of California

Gerard Brannon
Department of Treasury

Stanley Brytczuk
First National City Bank

Lewis H. Butler
Department of Health, Education and Welfare

Gail Cook
University of Toronto

André Danière
Boston College

William Friday
University of North Carolina

Kermit Gordon
President, The Brookings Institution

Samuel Halperin
Educational Staff Seminar

Martin Kramer
Department of Health, Education and Welfare

Harry Hogan
House Subcommittee on Higher Education

Robert W. Hartman
The Brookings Institution

Robert H. Haveman
Resources for the Future (now at the University of Wisconsin Institute for Research on Poverty)

Stanley J. Heywood
Eastern Montana College

Philip J. Hinson
Federal Reserve Bank of Boston

Carl Kaysen
Institute for Advanced Study

Lloyd A. Keisler
Indiana University

Clark Kerr
*Chairman, Carnegie Commission
on Higher Education*

John Mallan
*American Association of Junior
Colleges*

Arthur Marmaduke
*California State Scholarship
and Loan Commission*

Bernard Martin
Bureau of the Budget

John F. Morse
American Council on Education

Roger Noll
The Brookings Institution

Leif Muten
International Monetary Fund

James J. O'Leary
*United States Trust Company
of New York*

Joseph A. Pechman
*Director of Economic Studies
The Brookings Institution*

Allan W. Purdy
University of Missouri

Alice M. Rivlin
The Brookings Institution

Edward Sanders
*College Entrance Examination
Board*

Charles Saunders
*Department of Health, Education
and Welfare*

Norton Simon
Norton Simon, Inc.

Virginia Smith
*Carnegie Commission on Higher
Education*

William Vickrey
Columbia University

This book was set in Vladimir by University Graphics,
Inc. It was printed on permanent paper and bound by
The Maple Press Company. The designers were Elliot Epstein
and Edward Butler. The editors were Herbert Waentig and
Cheryl Allen for McGraw-Hill Book Company and Verne A.
Stadtman for the Carnegie Commission on Higher Education.
Frank Matonti and Alice Cohen supervised the production.

Hartman, Robert W
    Credit for college; public policy for student loans, by Robert W. Hartman. A report for the Carnegie Commission on Higher Education. New York, McGraw-Hill [1971]

    x, 152 p. illus. 24 cm. $5.95

    Bibliography: p. 115-120.

    1. Student loan funds—U.S. 2. Federal aid to higher education—U.S.   I. Carnegie Commission on the Future of Higher Education. II. Title.

LB2340.H36   379'.1214   75-158058
ISBN 0-07-010030-6   MARC

Library of Congress   71

10 (74